IRELAND
from the AIR

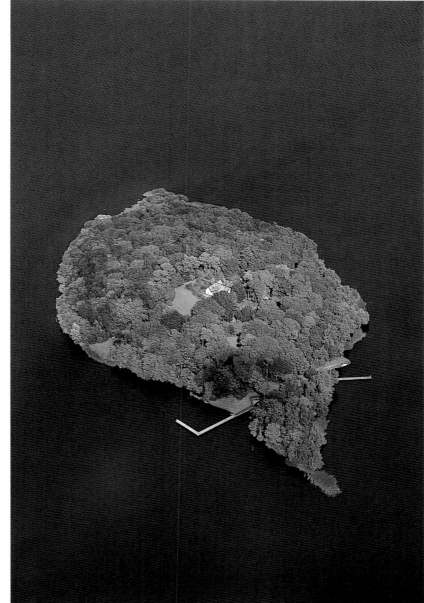

WHITE STAR
PUBLISHERS

IRELAND *from the* AIR

Photographs by
Antonio Attini

Text
Federica De Luca

Graphic Design
Paola Piacco

Translation
C.T.M., Milan

The publisher would like to
thank Bord Fáilte-The Irish
Tourist Board, particularly
Ciara O'Mahony, Jean Evans
and Peter Sherrard, and The
Northern Ireland Tourist Board,
especially Suzanne Murphy, for
their invaluable assistance.
The publisher would also like
to thank Aer Lingus for their
kind contribution to the
realization of this volume.

CONTENTS

ISBN 88-8095-508-X
23456 0504030201

Printed in Italy by
Rotolito Lombarda, Milan.
Color separations by
Bassoli, Milan.

1
Coalisland seems an
inaccessible, uninhabited,
drop-shaped island in the
center of the 154 square
miles of Lough Neagh.

2-3
One of the 2,500 peaceful
small lakes that dot the
countryside of central
Ireland in the counties of
Longford and Cavan.

4-5
Draped around the fort
built in 1650 by Colonel
Arthur Hill, Hillsborough is
one of the jewels of
Northern Ireland. A well-
cared for park with an
artificial lake hides a small
graveyard next to the
parish church where
Hamilton Harty, the
"Toscanini of Ireland", is
buried.

6 top
Along the shores of one of
the Lakes of Killarney, a
popular tourist destination
at the heart of Killarney
National Park.

6 bottom
Bantry, named after the heir
to the king of Ulster who
settled here in the first
century, has a French
connection.

7
A quarter of an hour by
car from Dublin, in
the peace of nearly 500
acres of park and an
exclusive golf course,
the angular Luttrellstown
Castle seems to come out
of a fairy tale. Here you
can make your fantasies
come true by renting
the castle, even for just
a day.

ireland

8 top left
The massive and solid Cliffs of Moher rise sheer from the sea off County Clare. Panoramic O'Brien's Tower stands at the top of the cliffs in the center of the photograph.

8 bottom left
An immense tableau of greens fills the mosaic of fields in the countryside of the Burren, giving equal prominence to large country houses and rustic farms.

8 top right
A skimming flight over the green sea off Mullaghmore Head reveals the ancient torpor that envelops the infrequent houses grouped around weatherbeaten churches above the fields.

10-11
A brightly-colored miniature shows the course of Donegal's Gweebarra river that descends from a valley surrounded by steep wilds close to Glenveagh National Park. The Park is one of Ireland's ten most visited spots.

INTRODUCTION

Ireland has one eye on America, which calls to her from across the Atlantic. The other is on Europe, to which she is anchored by a common history of interests, traditions, emigration, hardships and relationships that have accumulated over the centuries. She is suspended between two worlds to which, at heart, she feels she belongs. Without depending too much on either, that is how Ireland appears from the sky, an emerald-green ship adrift from the Old World, wrapped in a dimension that captures the soul of those who run to her with the same trust with which one would throw oneself into the arms of an old childhood nurse, capable of evoking memories of long forgotten fairy tales.

Even on your first encounter with Ireland, you will feel as if you have known her forever, like old school friends who meet up as adults and immediately re-establish their childhood relationships. Aerial photography is ideal for connecting old memories with what appears below us to be a miniature work of art, a unique combination of tranquility and restlessness. Stubborn yet fun, she winks at the prosperity that tourism has brought her over the last decade, though she has not subjected herself to the rules or compro-

mises that would suffocate her exceptional brand of individuality. Perhaps the recipe for her success lies in her innate independence; this allows her to remain exactly what she is and what so many before us have described in amazement, helping, though unaware, to spread her fame while at the same time falling prey to her charms.

It is a harmless weapon but one that has found many illustrious victims in this land that captivates the heart with fresh enthusiasm on every occasion, a land that breaks down all linguistic barriers with friendly smiles and shy greetings that invite any stranger to feel at home.

Ireland is the setting for holidays that supply fresh oxygen to the body and mind, that slip away day by day on a wave of emotions, marked by casual encounters sealed in a pub over glasses of Guinness or spontaneous conversations at the side of the road that follow no particular direction.

These are the preludes to nights spent in the peace of bed & breakfasts in the heart of the countryside, below velvet skies in the summer twilight that seem never to want to sleep but to preserve everything in a protective wrapping.

If such a thing as African sickness − the nostalgia for Africa − exists, then surely Irish sickness exists as well: a beneficial and contagious spell for which there are no remedies, that strikes the most sensitive of individuals, making them linger over small details, and live daily life free from anxiety in an old-fashioned land of small events and great people.

There are 26 counties in the Republic of Ireland shared among four provinces, and six counties in

12 top
Here we see the wide silvery bends of one of the six rivers that feed Lough Neagh, the basin ringed by five of Northern Ireland's six counties.

12 bottom
Calm waters and a low tide in Blacksod Bay provide the backdrop to

the rounded silhouette of The Mullet.

13
Dotted with small islands and its shores carved by small roads between the fields, Strangford Lough's connection with the sea means that its seemingly peaceful waters are fed by strong currents.

Northern Ireland. In all, less than 35,000 square miles in which to squeeze the personality of the island, to form the setting for its engrossing history, and to reveal all the thousands of tiny ways in which the intractable character of its people is manifested. It is a glorious epic of many chapters handwritten by poets and narrators, farmers and ranchers, the spirited depositories and defenders of an impenetrable language, Gaelic, that seems to hand down all the knowledge of the world.

Gaelic is the most authentic celebration of local culture, the banner of a people that describes itself as bilingual: English, of course, but especially Gaelic which proudly trumpets the country's divergence from the rest of the Anglo-Saxon world, the consequences of a history filled with suffering and trials but always faced with head held high. The people were proud even when the entire island was forced to capitulate to Fate and let its sons and daughters head overseas to the mysteries of an unknown Promised Land in order to create a new life for themselves after the Great Famine had decimated entire families and undermined all ambition.

In Ireland there is no need to search for Baroque architecture or great works of Renaissance art, nor to rush so as not to miss a visit to some museum or, above all, to make comparisons with other European countries and cultures.

Although the country has not forgotten its art and it has no lack of culture, its primary resources, at least those that this aerial perspective shows up most clearly, are quite different. And even if one only looks absent-mindedly, these treasures will surely present themselves.

What summarizes Ireland are, above all, the earth, the sea, the clean air, the rain that puts a gleam on everything and that pervading tranquility that infuses all with a simplicity so dignified as to disorient the visitor.

These are natural, almost primitive elements that form the ideal backdrop for escapes from the banal, and they leave everyone free to interpret and enjoy the sensations dictated by moods, fantasies and momentary atmospheres, but without commitment and with genuine pleasure.

Consequently, Ireland has always been a bountiful source of inspiration for plays, tales and novels throughout the history of literature. Its very landscape, every detail, every approach to life and its misfortunes have become the underlying themes of the works of its writers – writers who have left their mark, either committed to a personal internal search or acting as dogged combatants massed in support of freedom of speech and thought. Often, like ordinary people or, worse, as formidable wrongdoers, they were forced to flee into exile to defend their philosophy and choices in life. They were privileged and immortal figures, spokesmen for mysteries and events and anything related to this controversial land that could give them inspiration for a new plot: from politics experienced firsthand to the difficulties of youth, from the common events of everyday life to family stories, all themes described with authenticity, often from personal experience, and transferred to the page with freshness and humor.

This fervent creativity was rewarded four times with

the Nobel Prize for literature during the last century in well-deserved recognition of talents often brought to the fore by problem-racked lives lived in a sort of voluntary solitude and in declared disagreement with the atavistic Irish conventionality.

For example, the eccentric George Bernard Shaw, a shy and bashful Dubliner who had a difficult childhood, made his debut in the world of literature after trying a range of different jobs such as freelance journalist, music critic, and author of political manifestos. He moved to London when he was just 25 years old but his heart and mind never really left Ireland, and although dedicating just one full play and one single-act play to his country, he always thought of it as the land of his dreams and affections, and left generous donations to the National Gallery of Ireland in Dublin upon his death. His wealth was the fruit of his many successes on the greatest stages of the world with his shrewd anti-bourgeois plays.

Another Nobel Prize honored the innovative genius of Samuel Beckett, the Irish dramatist who opened new horizons in European theater in the 20th-century though he spent his life in France. The 1923 prize for literature was awarded to the poetry of the nostalgic William Butler Yeats, the decadent symbolist of the Celtic renaissance who was also a playwright and one of the founders of the Irish National Theatre. He too exiled himself in France, first in the

Norman department of Calvados and later on Cap Martin on the Côte d'Azur where he died. He was the most sincere voice of the magic of Sligo and of the liberty and independence of his homeland; he was rewarded with the Nobel Prize a year after being elected a Senator of the Free State of Ireland.

Last in the line of prize winners, Seamus Heaney from Northern Ireland represents a line of continuity from Yeats and is the modern heir to a literary culture that has its roots locked solidly in the sagas of Celtic heroes and in nature as a basis of life.

Nobel winners apart, Ireland can be proud as the birthplace of so many other writers, famous and less well-known, who have not only achieved success over the centuries in Irish and Anglo-Saxon literature, but have also made their mark on European art.

Another outstanding writer was Jonathan Swift, the author of *Gulliver's Travels*, who was considered the forerunner of James Joyce. Swift was one of the sharpest writers in the English language and had a streak of sarcasm that was truly ferocious. The son of English parents, he moved to London on completing his studies at Trinity College in Dublin but he did not find there what he had hoped for. Consequently, he accepted the invitation to return to what he had earlier described as "the most miserable country in the world" to live the rest of his life as the dean of St. Patrick's cathedral in Dublin.

By definition the land of "saints and scholars," Ireland has also been the mother of great sinners, whether real or presumed. Among the celebrities that have been rehabilitated and reassessed in modern times, Oscar Wilde, the symbol of dandyism, was the most outstanding victim of the morality of his age for which his fame was suffocated by scandals, trials and public censure. The shadow of sin was also cast over James Joyce, the bitter enemy of any type of convention who is now considered the most authoritative ambassador of erudite Ireland. He explored and immortalized unknown styles and languages and was the pioneer of completely new narrative techniques that revolutionized the literature of the early 20th-century. Joyce was a restless genius who turned to poetry after various attempts at the study of medicine. He left Ireland in 1902, seldom returning except for short periods. He lived in Paris and divided his time among short stories, novels and language teaching, later moving to Trieste where he struck up a close friendship with Italo Svevo, and finally to Zurich where he died in 1941. His long migration did not dim his memories of Dublin, which he always thought of as the starting point and goal of his literary journey.

But there were also less well-known names, such as the Dubliner James Stephens, a writer, journalist and long-time friend of Joyce, who drew on Ireland's heritage of myths, legends and medieval tales to reproduce them in fables. There was Sean O'Casey, the astute observer of human deeds and misdeeds who raised the level of Irish theater; and the learned scholars that were native to Ireland were joined by others from distant lands, sometimes to remain there drawn by her unending fascination. As the outline of the island begins to take shape before our eyes, this long, perhaps abstract literary discourse seems particularly suitable. It reminds us how the different means of artistic expression have always been nourished by Ireland and how they in

memories. Director John Ford made the ever-popular "The Quiet Man" starring John Wayne, which created the symbol of the obstinate yet ultimately good Irishman. John Huston, who directed "The Dead," used to spend long holidays in Ireland with his daughter, Angelica, during which he would bring together all the Hollywood stars of Irish origin. A new wave of cinematic stars has risen on the traces of the golden oldies including Jim Sheridan, Neil Jordan and films like "The Commitments" and the light-hearted "The Van." Then there are more intense films, appreciated by both the public and the critics, such as "My Left Foot" and the recent "Dancing at Lughnasa," but in particular there was "Michael Collins," the winner at the Venice Film Festival, passionately interpreted by the Northern Irish actor Liam Neeson. These films display cross-sections of a society that is sometimes paradoxical but always pervaded by a healthy sense of humor that remains the bulwark of emotions and rare principles. Most of all, however, these films display the places, roads and cities that cinematic fiction has made its own, thereby fostering the tourist trade across the whole island.

The sea that encloses it all within miles of beaches and jagged cliffs has always been the island's accom-

turn have always provided nourishment to the Irish in every age.

Literature is still one of the liveliest and most symbolic cultural forms in this land of five million inhabitants, three and a half million of whom live in the Republic. In this restricted society there are four national daily newspapers and buying a book is a common event, a collective passion. Literature is the subject of lively festivals, courses and seminars that regularly discuss the public and private lives of the country's most important figures from the past and present.

There has also been a growth in Irish cinema over the last decades, which has sympathetically drawn upon the wealth of Irish plays and novels in films made, and starred famous or emerging actors who more often than not have Irish blood in their veins. Many are emigrants from way back, either Irish by birth or second generation who return to the old country to relive something from their past or to find places about which they only retain distant

14
Patterns of blue and green frame the shores of Strangford Lough in Northern Ireland where "drumlins" (small hills created by sandy glacial deposits) take the form of unusual peninsulas.

15 top
This is the long shoreline of Tyrella Beach at the turning of the tide in County Down. It is a much-loved spot for horse riders who can go for long, open rides along the sheltered beach.

15 bottom
A section of the sandy shore of Blacksod Bay protected by a line of dunes and fields resembles a natural golf course – not unusual in Ireland.

plice and tyrant. Accomplice in the sense that it has allowed Ireland to preserve its unique values, tyrant for having made it the target of raiders and invading armies since the dawn of history. The invaders may have bent Ireland to their will from time to time but they never succeeded in breaking the pride or even scratching the integrity of its people.

First came the Celts, then the Vikings, the Anglo-Normans and, finally, the exhausting tussle with the English, who are as geographically close to the Irish as they are distant in character.

And even if, from up here in the clouds, we are unable to see the friendly smiles of people that have been fated not to take anything too seriously; and even if we are unable to understand the mysteries of the Celtic crosses carved with biblical symbols; and even if we are not aware of the smell of the wet earth and the burned peat, from this unusual viewpoint we are able to take everything in at a glance and enjoy landscapes immersed in a gentle, prolonged lethargy from which they have no wish to be roused.

The first sight of the island for those arriving from

continental Europe is the sinuous strip of land and sea wrapped around the Gaelic "Baile Átha Cliath" of King Conor Mac Nessa, renamed Dubh Linn, "Black Bog," by the Vikings. It was here this warrior people berthed their *drakar* − streamlined boats − on Ireland's marshy shores in the 11th-century and where they founded the cornerstone of their long conquest: Dublin, the beating heart and reference point of the Republic that is home to a large part of the population.

The city lies wrapped in a gray mantle, a gray that at first glance seems to cloak everything and induces sadness. The stones of the houses, the roofs, the flagstones in the streets, and even the sea to the west are all colored a dull leaden gray. As though it were wearing the uniform of an aristocratic school, Dublin wears the color of melancholy with extraordinary elegance, but despite this chromatic uniformity, the city soon shows it is filled with color and cheer. It is anything but nostalgic or phlegmatic; on the contrary, it is warm, filled with a genuine joie-de-vivre and a vitality that soon puts any stranger at ease.

A city with a Latin heart on the western fringe of Europe and for 800 or more years the center of the island's economic and political life, Dublin is an adult city with the spirit of a child. It feels like a provincial town but it has the ambitions of a capital that has grown up in the shadow of the rushed and impatient modern metropolises elsewhere on the continent. In Dublin, where one can enjoy oneself in a manner known in few other places in the world, extremes of all types exist together without compromise.

Young, informal and filled with life, the city is the benchmark for all that the new Ireland absorbs and assimilates from the rest of the world, while refusing to compromise its own character. In its own way, it is the trampoline for the avant-garde that aims to make its own mark on the worlds of fashion, design, music and every other artistic sphere.

A gift of nature due to the latitude the city lies on, Dublin's unreal light exalts the chessboard of open, well-delineated districts in the cityscape. It is an extensive city in which the buildings seldom exceed five stories and is threaded by the Liffey before it slides out into the Irish Sea. The Liffey is a band of liquid silver that marks the imaginary boundary between the north and south of the city, two ideologically and socially opposing, though complementary, entities that at one time only communicated over the iron Ha'Penny Bridge, named for the modest toll paid to cross to the other side.

The genuine, popular Dublin filled with the noise and action of everyday life lies along the north bank just over the wide O'Connell Street bridge and on either side of O'Connell Street itself. The area is a tangle of shopping streets ringing to the coarse shouts of

16 top
The compact bulk of the headquarters of the Garda, the Irish police, stands amid the extensive grounds of Phoenix Park, in Dublin. It is one of the few buildings inside the park along with the residence of the country's President and that of the Ambassador to the United States.

the merchants that animate Moore Street market just behind the austere building of the Central Post Office. This was the scene of the Easter Rising on April 24, 1916, when Michael Collins and his companions turned the centuries-old dispute with England into a declared challenge. This was the first official act in support of independence for the four provinces in the Republic of today, but it was to result in the open wound of the six Northern Irish counties hanging in the balance between war and peace.

Also on the north bank of the Liffey, almost on the edge of the city, lies Phoenix Park, the largest enclosed city park in Europe. Converted from a 17th-century hunting ground into a park open to the public in 1745, it is here that many Dubliners indulge their twin loves of nature and sport. Every Sunday the park hosts polo, cricket, and rugby matches and the public can take long walks or ride horses and

bikes through the avenues where it is not unusual to come across wild deer. Wandering among the centuries-old trees, you may find the lovely presidential residence named Áras an Uachtaráin and that of the American ambassador. Not far from the main entrance, a sequence of enclosures marks the site of the Zoo created in 1830. This is one of the few zoos in which the big cats still reproduce in captivity and can count among its number the roaring lions of Metro Goldwyn-Mayer.

Further north, near Croke Park, the stadium where the soccer hopes of a full-blooded sporting nation are raised, and near the area of Smithfield, the center of an urban recovery plan, stands a graceful conservatory on the green lawns of the Botanic Gardens, which were transformed from a private garden in 1795. It is famous for its collection of ancient roses and is affectionately considered by Dubliners as their "front garden."

The other side of the river is the cultivated and residential section of the city. It is a sequence of Georgian and Victorian townhouses in which the elegant Merrion Square and the more central St. Stephen's Green are situated. The latter is a 90,000 square meter park with fountains that lies alongside Grafton Street, the attractive pedestrian precinct lined by hotels, shopping centers, and luxury shops that forms one of the main means of access to Trinity College. The university was founded by Queen Elizabeth I in 1592 and is one of the most famous institutions in the capital. The academic focus in

Ireland, it has produced many scientists and men of letters. It is a temple of culture where great writers like Jonathan Swift, Oscar Wilde, Samuel Beckett and Bram Stoker (author of *Dracula*) passed their youth.

Surrounded by playing fields and avenues where the students spend their free time, the university is a city within a city, a tangle of dormitories, classrooms and laboratories that form offshoots to the Long Room, the library that holds volumes, manuscripts and valuable codices. It is home to the *Book of Kells*, a Gospel illuminated, in all probability, at Iona or Kells

18
Mullaghmore Bay, not far from Mullaghmore Cape, is one of the many examples of Ireland's primitive beauty. It offers a marvelous lookout over Donegal Bay.

19 top
Traces of "ring-forts," circular fortified enclosures, can still be seen in the hinterland of the Mullaghmore Bay. The forts were built thousands of years ago as shelters for livestock. Visitors are advised not to touch and especially not to take away a single stone from the structures or they will suffer misfortunes of all kinds!

by monks belonging to the order of St. Columban. It is a collection of parchment documents that shows how the task of illuminating the Roman-Christian world was carried out by Irish monks throughout Europe in the dark and changing times of the Middle Ages.

Faithful to the law of contrasts, Dublin counters the intellectual atmosphere of Trinity College with the entertainment district just a few steps away. The architecturally stern university lies on the edge of Temple Bar, the bubbling "Latin quarter" that was

scheduled to be demolished at the end of the 1980s to make way for a railway station. The local administration, however, had not foreseen the peaceful protest of the young, many of whom were students at Trinity, who convinced the authorities to revise their plans. Decked out in completely new guise under the dim lights of 19th-century streetlights, Temple Bar is a far-sighted example of urban renewal which has converted the interiors of deconsecrated churches and disused warehouses, while retaining their original styles, into recording studios, art galleries, fashionable hotels and guesthouses, and clubs where Celtic music merges with the rhythms of U2, The Chieftains and other great bands.

Beyond the square mass of Dublin Castle, the stronghold of British secular power for centuries, the Protestant cathedral of Christ Church at the far end of Dame Street is the home of Dublinia, an audiovisual show about Viking Dublin. If you should see huge carts pulled by draught horses, it is not a trick of your imagination: Dublin also counts these among its means of transport. Both a tradition and a custom that is hard to give up, the lumbering carts might be carrying tourists, barrels of beer or other types of goods.

Not far away on what used to be the boundary between the city and the districts of disrepute, stands St. Patrick's, another Protestant cathedral that has curiously become the principal religious center in this Catholic city. In the middle of a sprawl of red brick housing built by the democratic Guinness family to accommodate the workers from their factories, St. Patrick's marks the ancient city limit and the start of "The Liberties," an area of antique and craft shops, whose name refers to when it stood outside the city walls and was therefore free from taxation.

Flying over the last stretches of the south of the city, period houses and villas lie in ordered rows around

Baggot Street, the "in" area of Dublin, both sides of the city's watery belt of the Grand Canal. Soon after, a constellation of cheerful suburbs can be seen clustered along the seashore, including the busy Sandycove where quaint houses enjoy the sea breezes. Set on a narrow strip of land opposite Howth promontory on the edge of Dublin Bay, the stout Martello Tower is one of the many buildings constructed along the coast to defend against enemy attacks. For a while it was also home to James Joyce and since 1962 has been the site of the museum that bears his name. He only stayed there a short time but its importance lies in the fact that it was the setting for the first scene in his masterpiece, *Ulysses*. The book is the story of two men, Leopold Bloom, a middle-aged advertising man, and Stephen Dedalus, a young idealist poet, who set off at dawn on the

June 16, 1904 from this very tower on a trip to the city, just like a second Ulysses. This journey is relived each year on "Bloomsday" by tourists and locals who, with book in hand, retrace the most important sections of the day's trip, stopping off at the same places and reliving the same early-20th-century atmosphere minutely described in the book while surrounded by women in gloves and veils.

The last outreaches of the city to the south are the port of Dun Laoghaire, where Guglielmo Marconi made the first outdoor radio transmission in 1898, and Dalkey Island, where international stars of the cinema and music worlds choose to make their homes.

Like any capital, Dublin does not represent the entire country. It is the symbol of Ireland but at the same time it is its exact opposite, a center that keeps step with the rest of the world and acts as a marker for the country. Yet Ireland does not betray the customs and rhythms that represent the strength of a civilization still deeply rooted in agriculture. It presents itself to the world as a Celtic soul enveloped by nature; it is a country that likes to be watched and to be read like an open book, but to be read with the eyes and interpreted by the heart. This is the Ireland of dreams, myths and sacred silences to be absorbed and explored in the hope of finding something we might forever keep as a memory from this oral treasure.

The country is a palette of enamel colors that the

passing of the seasons highlights or dims without ever blemishing its natural beauty.

Not even bad weather wins out. Even when the sky is heavy and dull and the horizon portends the worst, the Irish do not speak of bad weather. This is the definition on which the German writer, Heinrich Böll, dwelled in his "Diary of Ireland," playing down its effects: "To call rain bad weather would be disproportionate, like calling good weather the sun at its peak, dazzling... It is simply weather and it reminds us expressly that its element is falling water." When not referring to the harsh wind, "bad weather" in Ireland signifies "soft rain," the gentle but continuous drizzle that soaks to the bone and gives the land those tones of green that painters find difficult to imitate. It does not even discourage the tourists to whom, anywhere else in the world, this phenomenon would certainly constitute a nuisance. The rain is an

occasional traveling companion in the sense that the green of the countryside is a sort of Virgil that accompanies us on our journey throughout the island. And, perhaps if the rain did not exist, it would be necessary to invent it to enjoy to the maximum the sense of peace diffused by the Irish landscape that wafts the perfumes of wild essences to us with every breath.

The ancient horse-racing course, the Curragh, stretches away to the south of the curve of the Grand Canal. Its green expanses were recently borrowed for the shooting of epic battle scenes for the film "Braveheart" and are the visitor's introduction to the extensive grasslands of County Kildare. This traditional horse-breeding area is home to the National Stud at Tully, the national stables where some of the world's greatest champions have been bred.

Nearby, the Japanese Gardens, one of the most beautiful oriental gardens in Europe and unusual at this latitude, speaks to us with its mystical and symbolic language. Next door, a new park has been created, dedicated to St. Fiachra.

This is the beginning of another Ireland, a starting point for a journey along which there will be few large towns, a journey in which the recurring ele-

20 top
A handful of houses and a few, sparsely traveled roads. These signs of man's discreet and respectful presence soften the coastline of Donegal Bay without spoiling its primitive beauty.

20 bottom
Fishing boats of all nations wait to head out to sea once more at the wharves of Killybegs harbor on the coast of County Donegal. This is one of the largest fishing centers on the island and in all of the north Atlantic.

21
Close to the coast and the village of Fenit, the white lighthouse on the small island of Little Samphire watches over the entrance to Tralee Bay, capital of the popular tourist area of County Kerry.

ment is color. At times absolute and defined, at others merged into gradations in which it is difficult to identify the dominant shade, an immense patchwork appears, irregularly sewn together by narrow country roads, stone walls, bushes whipped by gusts of sea wind, and rivers of flashing salmon. The landscapes throughout the country are similar overall but differ in the proportions of the elements that compose them.

Given that Ireland offers up to 40 shades of green, it is not surprising that this color is the unquestioned lord of County Wicklow, a rolling sequence of gentle hills. Here we find the crumbling ruins of Glendalough, our first encounter with the Ireland of the saints, almost hidden in a small valley bejewelled with streams and small lakes. Between rises in the land that yearn to be mountains, the Wicklow Gap traces a path in a primordial land not far from Wicklow National Park.

This is an area forgotten by the major routes but one that delights the visitor with views of ancient trees and brightly colored flowerbeds. These are the local results of the 18th-century passion for landscape gardening in which owners of large estates, wishing to create beauty while also displaying their extravagance, went further than building, rebuilding or redecorating their magnificent country residences. Even the frame of the picture had to reflect one's social status and to match the tastes of the age. And so, just as painters attempt to imitate nature as faithfully as possible, landscape artists began to emulate painters in a mix somewhere between simplicity and poorly concealed ostentation. The result is that County Wicklow is dotted with country houses surrounded by centuries-old parks and gardens that Patrick Bowe, a botanical expert, defined as, "Wild, like the Irish themselves." Although, rather than wild, they are simply undomesticated, left mostly to grow as they please and curtailed only by the moods of the climate.

The lovely estate of Powerscourt lies at the foot of the recently restored 18th-century building ravaged by fire in the 1970s. This is the best-known estate in

the county and the largest on the entire island; it was redesigned in the second half of the 19th-century in accordance with the popularity of French and Italian styles. A colorful mix of paths leads between beds of rhododendrons, flights of steps and stone fountains as far as the natural gallery that overlooks the Dargle valley. From here the garden seems to throw itself into the void as a waterfall sparkles over 300 feet to the valley bottom.

There are impressive areas of land that are more to be experienced than admired, sometimes created to commemorate the dead who honored the mother country abroad. This is the case with the John F. Kennedy Memorial Arboretum that was inaugurated in 1968 near Dunganstown, the village from which the great grandfather of the future President Kennedy of the United States emigrated. Wishing to commemorate a visit made by Kennedy to Ireland a few months before his assassination, the arboretum was preferred by the Irish communities of America to a stone memorial or banal monument in order to symbolically represent their illustrious fellow countryman in life. In consequence, they subsidized the creation of this nursery, today open to the public, that is home to more than 4,500 species of plants and trees from the five continents.

In Ireland the past is equally as vivid as the present and in more than one instance forms a bridge to the future. One example is given by nearby Wexford, the capital of Wexford county, where the first treaty with the English was signed in 1169 in the ruins of

Selskar Abbey. The past of this small town, founded by the Gauls, is related both to the deeds of the Vikings and to Ireland's third language, great music. Each autumn, the town mounts an operatic festival in which rare compositions by famous composers and stage settings that have long remained unseen are put on display.

On the southeast tip of the island in St. George's Channel, Rosslare looks towards the coast of France. From afar, the ferry connections between the two seem to be an exchange of favors between neighbors and represent an unconscious opportunity to perpet-

22 left
The rounded mound over the tomb at Newgrange is the main sign of the existence of a necropolis dating from 3200-2700 BC. The necropolis is spread over an area of 5 miles near Drogheda in the county of Meath.

22 right
The stone ring at Carrowmore Bronze Age Cemetery lies south of the town of Sligo. This is only one of the many sections of the largest megalithic complex in Ireland and the second largest in Europe. So far roughly 60 tombs and dolmens have been discovered.

uate and cement distant relationships.

Waterford, which lends its name to the largest crystal factory in the world, tucked in an opening on the Suir estuary, and Dunmore East, at the head of the bay, also evoke the Ireland of the past with tiny villages of thatched cottages.

A short deviation inland before continuing on the clockwise circuit of the island brings us to Tipperary, where the spectacular Rock of Cashel rises dramatically amidst the fields. The Rock is a sentinel that has watched over the traffic between Dublin and Cork for centuries and, like Glendalough, is another instance of the monastic life that the soldiers of Cromwell reduced to ruins.

But the force of arms and fire did not succeed in completely destroying the imposing building where, on the crest of the green hill, a collection of Celtic crosses, small churches and empty towers still rises towards the sky. Seemingly mystical and sinister, they communicate an aura of holiness that we will

23 top
The entrance to the tomb at Newgrange below the grass and moss opens into a passageway about 20 yards long that leads to the burial chamber itself. Once a year, on December 21, the winter solstice, the sun's rays enter the tomb for just 17 minutes.

23 bottom
Here is an unusual view of the hill of Knocknarea not far from the Sligo Bay. It is said that the legendary Maeve, Queen of Connacht in the 1st century AD, is buried under the prehistoric mound here, known as Knocknarea Cairn.

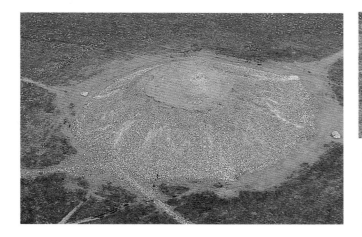

find several more times on this journey.

Gradually the eye begins to linger on signs of a rural and seafaring world made up of small details that represent an unchanging routine. It was in this area that the island experienced one of the saddest periods in its difficult history, the Great Famine, caused in the second half of the 19th-century by a mysterious parasite that destroyed the potato crops which made up a substantial part of the Irish diet for centuries. The Famine initiated a massive depopulation of the island through death and emigration that for many began at the port of Cobh, a busy harbor town

that faces and almost challenges Cork, the town that was built on the "Corcaigh," the marshland of the Lee estuary. The second largest city in the Republic and a university town, Cork is more distinguished for its cultural vitality and the quality of its art galleries in the Huguenot quarter than for its architecture. Its single point of reference is St. Finbarr's church around which the city seems to radiate with its Victorian townhouses in pink stone and the buildings on Grand Parade and St. Patrick's Street. These two large streets, filled with shops, open onto the wide vaults of the Old English Market where one can taste "crúibíns" (pigs' trotters), "drisheen" (black pudding), handmade cheeses and a thousand delicacies from land and sea. And these two streets boast the highest concentration of pubs per square foot anywhere on the island! This is a difficult record to

For centuries a landmark for pilgrims and travelers, the imposing fortress that is the symbol of County Tipperary, the Rock of Cashel, was the

stronghold of the Irish resistance around 1000 AD. The Round Tower stands above while Cormac's Chapel lies behind the wall in the foreground.

25 top
Adare Manor, built between 1832-76 on the river Maigue in County Limerick, is now one of Ireland's most exclusive hotels.

achieve but perfectly reflects the agricultural nature and rustic customs of the region.

A recent survey has put the number of pubs throughout the country at 11,000. They are a real social institution, a place for meeting people, conducting business, whiling away the time in chat, and for musical evenings that conjure up images of singing in the America of the pioneers. Pubs are the place where many Irish eat a light midday meal of soup, sandwiches with a glass of beer, of course, and where baptisms and weddings are celebrated with the same enthusiasm as a victory by the local sports team.

Just as Wicklow is known as the garden of Ireland, Cork is its orchard, its most representative gastronomic region and the home of internationally renowned cuisine.

Cork is where the full flavors of old-style cooking are based on the produce of the sea: fresh oysters, shellfish and tasty slices of smoked salmon to be eaten with buttered soda bread and accompanied by a stout or two. However, these are just mouthwatering snacks and detract nothing from traditional recipes like hearty soups and Irish stew made from lamb, potato and vegetables in typical country style, cooked for hours over the heat of an ancient stove.

Flying over the suburbs of Cork, we can see an enormous still, perhaps the largest in the world, which indicates the Midleton distillery and perfectly represents the passion for whiskey the Irish share with their cousins the Scots. Whiskey in Ireland is only second to beer and forms one of the prime ingredients for Irish coffee, the rich mixture of coffee, whiskey and cream invented 50 years ago by a bartender at Shannon airport.

Protected by the bastions of Charles Fort and James Fort, Kinsale is the flower in the buttonhole of west Cork. It is the picturesque Irish equivalent of Portofino and tempts one to stop off at one of its many restaurants to try the famous seafood, to take to the sea in a sailboat, or to lose oneself in the little streets full of pastel-colored houses, which were restored in the 1970's.

From here, the coast stretches along the ocean like an open hand as though it were trying to grab all the warm currents of the Gulf Stream. At Skibbereen, we find the "Ring of Kerry," one of the most popular tourist circuits for its rare loveliness, stretching down to Baltimore and the rocky Clear Island. This is the southernmost point of the Republic and lies just a few miles from Fastnet Rock, where a lighthouse signals the rounding of the mark in the Fastnet sailing race, held each year since 1925.

A strip of land sticks out along the jagged coastline before reaching Bantry Bay, the home of superb oysters. The little port of Glengarriff is the point of departure for a short trip, under the incredulous gaze of seals and penguins guided here by the warm currents, to Garinish Island with its subtropical gardens in the middle of the bay.

This short trip is just a teaser for the breathtaking loveliness provided by the Skelligs, three protected islands nine miles from Iveragh peninsula where sea birds have found a safe refuge. Impressive to look at but a fragile habitat, the islands are a wonderful nature reserve that were in part populated by monks from the 7th to the 13th centuries. Traces of the distant past can be seen in the pre-Norman steps, terracing, chapels and rustic accommodations among the windswept rocky heights of Skellig Michael, the largest of the three islands.

Fresh and salt water form a filigree on the land below. A lacework of rivers, lakes and rounded hills surround Killarney, a small town popular with tourists, and the Killarney National Park. Towards the Atlantic, the land seems to fray and break into a thousand inlets before reaching the tip of the world at Dingle, a 16th-century fishing town protected by rugged hills and lauded in the tales of old sailors. Not far away, Dunmore Head, the westernmost tip of Ireland, is the last land before the Americas. The stretch of water in front of Great Blasket Island was the setting for the shipwreck of several of the ships belonging to King Philip's invincible Armada in 1588. From here the coast folds back on itself to enter the large mouth of the Shannon estuary that separates County Clare from County Limerick. The Shannon forms the spine of the island and is the longest river in the British archipelago. It rises on the slopes of the Cuilcagh mountains and flows 230 miles to the Atlantic, connecting the most inland areas via canals and lakes where the first religious communities sprung up.

For the most part navigable, the Shannon was for centuries the main means of transit and sometimes of escape in a rocky country with few communication routes, and thus it was a natural resource to be defended using every means. It was on the banks of this river – now plied by tourist boats and visited by thousands of species of migrating birds from all over north Europe and Greenland – that forts, military bases and countless monasteries were built in bygone ages.

Traveling upstream, we soon come across Clonmacnoise, the geographical heart of the country and one of the loveliest examples of the Ireland of the saints. Today a national museum, it was founded in 545 by St. Ciaran on the left bank of the middle stretch of the river at Esker Riada, the limestone outcrop that marked the passage of pilgrims heading towards the capital during the Middle Ages. Several times attacked by Vikings and Normans, the monastery today is what remains of the glorious site destroyed by the English in 1552: towers, crosses, monolithic crosses with elaborate bas-reliefs, roofless churches and chapels are reminders of the pious figures to whom Ireland owes some of its most profound debts of gratitude. They were the religious figures who founded the deep and unswerving loyalty of the Irish to St. Patrick, the founding father of entire dynasties of preachers and founder of the Armagh monastery, whose memory is celebrated on March 17 wherever in the world there is an

25 bottom
The spectral ruins of Dunluce Castle, the 14th-century manor overlooking the rocky slopes of Antrim in Northern Ireland, was rebuilt on several occasions. Home to the MacDonnell clan and the center of numerous struggles between the noble families of Ulster, it was destroyed by a severe storm that practically flattened it.

At the end of the bay that bears its name, Bantry is a manufacturing and tourist town famous for the attempts of the French republican fleet to land there in 1796. Bantry House was opened in 1992, following the discovery of the wreck of the French frigate "La Surveillante."

27

Pleasure boats and sailboats lie berthed in the picturesque harbor of Kinsale, a well-known sailing and fishing center near Cork, where the Bandon river meets the sea.

Irish community.

The son of a Roman noble and perhaps born in Wales with the Celtic name of Succat, according to legend Patrick was captured at the age of 16, carried off to Ireland and sold to an Irish chief called Milchu. After two escapes, Patrick went to France where he became a monk and eventually a bishop at the age of 45. Sent by Pope Celestine I to Ireland as a missionary in 432, he introduced Christianity to the land where he remained until his death. His followers took their faith throughout Europe to brighten the glow of a religion that had been greatly dimmed and founded monasteries in Meux in France, San Gallo in Switzerland, Wurzburg in Germany and as far south as Bobbio in Italy, which is still linked to the work of St. Columban.

These are true stories of a lighthearted country that likes to play hide-and-seek with its memories. It loves to lace truth with imagination and documented proof with invention, sometimes more surprising than reality. This is the case of the 15th-century Bunratty castle to the northwest of Limerick where true-to-life medieval court banquets are re-enacted among Celtic melodies and the rustle of brocade. A similar lightning-quick trip into the past can be had at the Folk Park, a playful but educational reconstruction of Irish country villages from the 18th-century. The smells of freshly baked bread and spices recall past livelihoods in a bustle of shopkeepers, farriers and cobblers wearing period dress. The living

past goes even deeper at Craggaunowen where camps of reed and straw huts reconstruct the ways of life of the Bronze Age and the customs of the Celts.

Before returning to the coastal route, Limerick is well worth a glance. A Viking city on the river Shannon, it was destroyed after the battle of Clontarf and rebuilt to become the residence of the King of Munster. It is a town with two souls, one Irish and the other English, whose historical vicissitudes meet in King John's Castle, a fortified citadel built in the 13th-century that today houses an interesting museum. The town is also known for its excellent lace and the quality of its smoked ham.

Gradually, the ocean becomes wider and flocks of gannets and puffins become our companions on this high-altitude journey. Sometimes, they join up with herring gulls, the sentinels of the Cliffs of Moher, a five-mile barrier of cliffs that withstands the incessant violence of the Atlantic waves. Theirs are the calls that guide us through the early morning mists over the rainbow to where the leprechauns have hidden their legendary pots of gold in one of the many beliefs that Ireland loves to hand down from generation to generation. Hymns to Irish history and civilization, the extraordinary adventures of elves and wizards held only in the collective memory are passed down through the generations by word of mouth by the "Seanchaí," the storytellers that move from village to village, especially in the less populated regions to the west, enchanting entire families in front of a fire during long evenings.

The latest generation of gypsies or, more correctly, travelers seems to turn these legends into reality as they move from place to place in their caravans, not following any schedule but simply on the lookout for a job.

Many Irish women wear gold and silver jewelery in the forms of harps or Celtic effigies, in particular the

"Claddagh Ring," a ring that depicts a heart topped by a crown and held in two open hands. Look in which direction the tip of the heart is pointing to know if the woman who wears the ring is married or has a heart free from commitments.

Overcoming any desire on our part to follow a route decided at the drawing board, it is the natural marvels of Ireland that decide the direction of our flight, taking us now to the wonders of the Burren, the wilder side of County Clare. This is a gigantic and geologically important limestone plateau that eventually tips precipitously into the ocean. Each Spring it is covered by spectacular blooms of wild orchids and other botanical rarities.

The name of the most authentic gateway to the west is Galway, derived from Princess Galvia. Founded by kled at random by an invisible hand; each home is the setting for the intimacy of the family which, for every Irishman, remains unquestionably the most important value in the land.

This is the Ireland of tiny streams that hide from view, then reappear with all their silvery vigor, of narrow twisting roads marked by crossroads and unintelligible road signs, and of sheep that wander between the tweed-colored fields and skip along the side of the road each time a car passes or at any sound that disturbs the unreal tranquillity.

In the middle of this peace, charming farmhouses, elegant country houses and imposing castles appear amid the greenery. Whether historical mansions or simply old buildings, they are the symbol of Irish hospitality capable of combining the simplicity of a

Norman knights, it is the first stop on a journey to the far west of Ireland. It was a university town as long ago as the 14th-century and had strong trading relations with Spain that gave it a certain distinction and a propensity for business. Galway lies at the edge of the poignant solitude of Connemara that becomes apparent as soon as one leaves the city.

Cerulean lakes set like precious stones among the meadows ripple in the wind and reflect thousand-year old abbeys, brambles and dry-stone walls that divide the countryside into squares like handkerchiefs of land, each passed down through generations. Once more, a symphony of colors and rural fragrances are the background to slow whorls of smoke that rise from the cottages seemingly sprin- stay in a family with the privileges of a holiday spent with a noble family. The best opportunity for falling prey to temptation is first thing in the morning, with a revitalizing breakfast difficult to refuse even by those accustomed to a cup of coffee and a croissant in some anonymous bar. Here you enjoy fresh milk, bacon and eggs, warm toast and marmalade, and homemade cakes to be dunked in tea or coffee. Select what you like and eat at leisure at tables in small rooms heated by a fire, under the placid eyes of sheep and their lambs wandering in the fields outside the windows.

Often buffeted by heavy storms, the Aran Islands appear off to our left. Inishmore and her sisters Inishmaan and Inisheer are three small worlds to themselves where life moves to the rhythm of bicycle pedals or the clip clop of draught horses hooves or perhaps the swashing of the sea against the sides of the "currachs," the traditional fishing boats made from tarred planking. The only motors are those of the tractors on Inishmore, the largest of the three islands, but in spite of small concessions to modernity, the islands remain a favorite destination of tourists who obstinately wish to associate the image of the entire country with sweaters made from coarse wool decorated with patterns of a thousand meanings, and rough caps worn by sailors or farmers whose faces might have been carved from wood.

And though simplified, this is yet another confirmation of how much Ireland likes to remain snug and secure in those certainties that have become commonplace and which do not require explanation: merits and defects that give it its charm and humanity, the foundations of its silent landscapes that are so difficult to leave, landscapes capable of catalyzing the forces and attention of those who wish to discover the country's most hidden corners as they linger in flight over the coast of northwest Ireland search-

ing for new horizons to explore.

Maybe this is the least obvious and most intense area of the country, able to astound even the most experienced of travelers with a particular slant of the light that breaks the smooth monotony of the countryside. It may be motionless but it is able to inspire in the spectator an extraordinary vital force and arouse buried feelings and that childlike sense of candor often difficult for an adult to retrieve.

These are landscapes from which ballads played on flutes and Celtic harps burst forth spontaneously, at first just heard, then with more emphasis to the rhythm of pipers and the deep beats of the "bodhráns," the goatskin drums.

Voices join in, that seem to come from the beginning of time, associated with the holiness of places that lie off the beaten track and which one comes across

now and then quite by chance. These are places that leave a sense of surprise and which are difficult to forget, like Croagh Patrick, the holy mountain just outside Westport, an aristocratic little town designed by James Wyatt, the fashionable architect during the Georgian period. A small chapel can be seen on the peak of the mountain, the destination of pilgrims that gather at the end of July to celebrate the sermons of St. Patrick and his deeds to rid the island of reptiles and poisonous animals. And if, when considering his feats, you are prey to doubts as to what is faith and what is simply popular belief, just look around over Clew Bay, to the lighthouse on Clare Island and the mass of Achill Island to consider whether the future patron saint of Ireland found here the right place for one of his miracles.

Achill is the largest of the islands that ring Ireland and is the land of the purest Gaeltacht. It gave up its geographical isolation about a century ago but the bridge that joins it to the mainland has not changed the island's retiring nature. Its roads spread like rivulets in a thousand directions between houses and small graveyards. The prettiest route of all, which from above seems like a thin ribbon of iridescent satin, is the Atlantic Drive that runs up the west coast, silhouetting the land against the deep blue of the restless ocean that forms an omnipresent background to existences based on the rituals of farming and fishing or on maintaining the remains of archaeological settlements and megalithic tombs. Such settings suggested novels to authors like Graham Greene and Heinrich Böll. The German, in fact,

bought a house at Dugort in 1958 where he spent long periods during the last years of his life.

The lighthouse on the small island of Achillbeg at the extreme south tip of Achill Island gazes across the stretch of water that separates it from Clare Island and over Clew Bay to Croagh Patrick. The tower of Carrick Kildavnet Castle evokes the memory of its 16th-century owner, Grace O'Malley, the daughter of the chief of the O'Malley clan and undisputed tyrant of the west coast of Ireland. Following the early death of her husband, Grace took command of a band of pirates but was captured and fell into the hands of the English. It is said that her passionate defiance even conquered the heart of the feared Queen Elizabeth I and that for this audacity she was rewarded with her life, but her spirit was never at rest and there are those who believe she still haunts the ruins of what used to be the stronghold of her power. But then this is yet another myth in a country that loves to embroider and overlay facts to give history its true role.

The outline of the desolate, bare lands of the north drowsing below a cover of heather and moss can be made out between the galloping clouds. The vegetation is laid like a soft shawl over the peat where the houses, fields and tombs of the Ceide Fields, a farming colony established in the Stone Age, have for thousands of years dominated the natural terrace overlooking the shores of County Mayo.

This land is a rural painting like so many of the others we have already seen but it is unique, set in time and difficult to imitate, perfect for the innate poetry of nearby Sligo, loved by Yeats who is buried at Drumcliff, the small graveyard that lies below the imposing, flat-topped rise of Benbulben.

Then there is Donegal, homeland of Enya and bogs fringed by bays and inlets that provide refuge to the large fishing boats of Killiybegs manned by sailors that seem the direct descendants of Captain Ahab. Flat expanses break up into the tiny scales of The Rosses, uninhabited cliffs that emerge from the sea at Dunglow, and then, offshore, the huge rock named Tory Island rises from the sea like a giant. A rebellious and contradictory region, Donegal is the most Irish in nature of them all. It is a blend of the mild and the wild where man only rarely appears but, however desolate, it has never lost its sense of identity: it was the only county in Ulster to pass to the Republic in 1922 out of the British dominion. Surrounded by deep, long uninhabited valleys that have partly been turned into nature reserves, it is home to Glenveagh National Park which since 1975 has protected the steep slopes that flank the shores of Lough Veagh and the course of the Glenveagh river. Geography knows neither religion nor politics and soon we pass over the border into Northern Ireland,

28 left
Coolbanagher Church is the pride and joy of the village of Coolbanagher a few miles north of Port Laoise. It is a Protestant church that was built in Neoclassical style in 1786 from a design by James Gandon, one of Ireland's most important architects.

28 top right
Pure Neoclassical lines mark Emo Court, originally the residence of the counts of Portarlington and later turned into a Jesuit college.

28 bottom right
The cradle of Celtic Ireland, central County Meath is sprinkled with rural churches hidden in copses. Once a religious and cultural center, the region now focuses on agriculture and livestock.

29
Narrow strips of land and elegant promontories line the shores of Lough Neagh. In summer, the waters of the lake are plied by tourist boats from Antrim.

the part of the country that still suffers the consequences of the historic conflict with England and which was racked by decades of terrorism that relegated the country into a sort of limbo. It is now gradually leaving that tunnel and proclaiming its desire to live and to offer the best of itself as a natural continuation of a journey started in its blood relation, the Republic of Ireland.

In fact the countryside does not change a great deal. The coastline is more compact perhaps, but just as attractive. Heading in the direction of Belfast, the spectacular ruins of the 16th-century Dunluce Castle dominate the sea near Portrush. This romantic fort was built on a slope 30 meters high and naturally isolated from the mainland by a series of natural channels but also overlooking the extraordi-

nary rock formation between Runkerry and Dunseverick known as the Giant's Causeway. This amazing natural feature consists of 40,000 hexagonal basalt columns formed by an eruption sixty million years ago. Naturally, the phenomenon is accompanied by a legend that says the rocks are what remains of the path built by the giant Finn Mac Cool to reach Ireland from Scotland without having to get his feet wet in the cold waters of the North Channel.

From one marvel to another: Carrickarade Bridge near Ballintoy seems a bridge of sighs, a floating gangway suspended 30 meters above the sea to unite the mainland with the small island of Carrickarade.

The name Belfast originates from "Béal Feirste," Gaelic for "ford of sand." The city's verdigris dome over City Hall and its red brick suburbs are characteristic of any modern city. Unlike its rival Dublin, which flourished during the Industrial Revolution, Belfast, home to the weaving and shipbuilding industries, welcoming pubs and bizarre churches, is now back on the upswing. The city has been given the responsibility for guiding the future of this young country of ideas and spirit and for the education of its future leaders, whose task it will be to re-

store trust throughout the island in the country's ability to negotiate a peaceful future.

Northern Ireland's future leaders may attend the lovely Queen's University founded in 1845 which, along with the universities of Cork and Galway, constituted the third royal education institute in the country. This state of affairs lasted until 1908 when Queen's passed to the state.

Belfast still shows signs of the years it spent in fear but already presages a slow but progressive transformation. It is a port of strategic importance at a world level and intends to return to the glory of the years in which the shipbuilder's yard Harland and Wolff saw the construction of the Titanic and which, until the 1980's, boasted the largest cranes in the world, nicknamed David and Goliath.

As we head south towards Dublin, the last standing remains of Mellifont Abbey can be seen in the

30 left
The long journey of the cobalt waters of the Gweebarra river, which winds between fields and sand banks from the hills of the Inishowen peninsula to the Atlantic, is one of the wonders of northern Donegal.

30 right
The ruins of the Franciscan Friary founded in 1464 by the Fitzgerald family stand in the lushness of the golf course at Adare Manor. The round tower seems almost intact and is surrounded by the remains of chapels, the choir, the cloister and the tombs of the family.

31

The landscape of County Down in Northern Ireland is marked by rises of gravel and sand formed by the melting of the glaciers during the Ice Age.

Boyne valley, inland from Drogheda. Founded in 1142, Mellifont was the first Cistercian monastery in Ireland but was turned into a fortified residence in 1539. A few miles further south, an extraordinary necropolis older than the Egyptian pyramids will leave an indelible memory. This is Newgrange where about 30 "passage graves" spread across five miles form one of the most important prehistoric monuments in Europe. Once a year, on December 21 – the winter solstice – a slender shaft of sunlight enters the gloom of the narrow burial chamber for 17 minutes.

The wind that bustles the strings of clouds ceaselessly on also pushes us south. Below, in contrast to the blue of the sky, there are the changing colors of the bays of Dundalk and Carlingford filled with oysters and shellfish, the trout-filled lakes of the inland counties of Meath and Westmeath, the vivid green of the forests and the dark streaks of the peat bogs that cover a seventh of the entire island. These were a precious resource to the country that till just a few decades ago was called the "Cinderella of Europe." At one time these bare expanses of water and vegetable sediments were used as grazing land and its covering as fertilizer for fields or bedding for livestock, then its value as a fuel was discovered. Even today it is not unusual to see clumps of sod drying out close to the edge of the road waiting to be taken to domestic fires. Similarly, they are used for the production of energy in power stations as government directives have emphasised the use of environmental resources as much as possible.

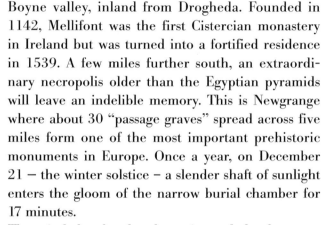

Our journey comes to an end as the coastline becomes more uniform and flatter. Pleasant towns like Skerries, Swords, and Howth spring up that live in the reflected light of the nearby capital: Howth with its steep and narrow streets offers a splendid view over Dublin Bay and Lambay Island where the small ports are lined with grounded boats awaiting high tide to take them back to sea for the next catch.

The threads of the fairways of Portmarnock golf course, one of 340 courses across the island, and the long avenues that lead to Malahide castle are the last visual flash on the flight you wish would never end. The circle has closed and the journey around the island is complete, at least as far as the salient points are concerned. On the way back from the airport, you feel lighter and more of a dreamer, filled with an experience that will be much more than a simple memory.

Having arrived on the island a little unsure, convinced you would not be able to understand its many mysteries, you leave Ireland as a friend and already with a sense of nostalgia. Nostalgia for the warm reception you were given, for that something that cannot be put into words but which you know you are leaving behind and you wish could be crystallized forever. You experience a stupefaction that has all the symptoms of a minor ailment but one you do not wish to fight. It will become a reassuring refuge over the days to come and will help shelter you from any restlessness. It is a virus that we had expected from the very beginning of the trip, a combination of witchcraft and enchantment that touches your heart, inviting you to discover yourself a little.

Call it Irishmania or Irelandesia. The important thing is that it never goes away.

32-33
The power of the Atlantic cuts the coast of Kerry into a lovely sequence of gulfs and bays. This is the prelude to one of the most authentic areas of Ireland, the Gaeltacht, where Gaelic traditions are most evident.

KERRY
NATURE AT THE FORE

33
Small boats navigate the mouth of the bay that leads into the natural harbor of Dingle. The area is known for being the home of Fungie, a dolphin that likes to perform for tourists in the summer.

34-35
The landscape bears a resemblance to stretches of Canada with the crystalline waters of the Lakes of Killarney formed by three bodies of water: the Leane, the Upper and Muckross lakes connected by twisting streams. Together the three form a quarter of Killarney National Park.

32 bottom
Near Ballyferriter on the winding Kerry coastline, a spur of rock sticks out into the sea marking the westernmost point of all Europe. Ballyferriter is also famous as a link to one of the last local princes to be defeated by the English in the 16th-century.

36 top
Innisfallen is the largest island in Lake Leane which is, in turn, the largest of the three lakes that form the Lakes of Killarney. The photograph shows the thick forest of oak and other tall trees that cover the entire island.

36 bottom
Tourist boats wait for passengers at the Innisfallen wharf. The ruins of a church founded by St. Finan in the 7th-century stand on the island that can be reached from Killarney by chartered boats.

36-37
The ruins of an ancient abbey
stand among the holes on
Adare Manor golf course.
The town of Adare, known for
its thatched cottages, was
built by the Normans who
founded new religious orders
and re-established stability in
a system that was running out
of control.

37 bottom
The wood on Innisfallen is a
rarity in that it is a
throwback to Ireland's
original appearance. The
forests of the country were
cut down by the English for
two reasons: for trade and,
more importantly, so that
Irish rebels would have fewer
hiding places.

38-39
Green and blue blend
perfectly to form one of the
inlets of Dingle Bay and the
outline of the Dingle
peninsula, the northernmost
of the three promontories in
County Kerry.

39 bottom
The sparse white houses in
the fields that stand over the
bare cliffs of the Dingle
peninsula look towards
Skellig Rocks and the
Blasket Islands in the
Atlantic Ocean.

39 top
The Mediterranean
landscape and deep blue
sea of Dingle Bay offer safe
shelter to dozens of tourist
boats.

40-41
The wild beauty of the
Dingle peninsula is matched
by its more than 2,000
archaeological sites dating
from the Iron Age to the late
Middle Ages, most of which
require further research and
exploration.

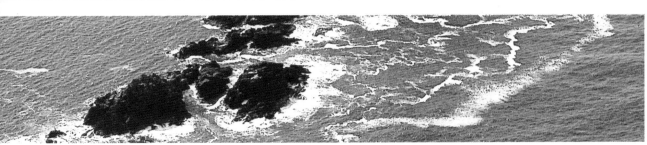

42 top
Foaming waves form a delicate lacework around the rocks off Doulus Head, which marks the tip of the south shore of Dingle Bay and the north side of the famous Ring of Kerry.

42 bottom
In silhouette, the coast of Kerry looks like a soft cushion embroidered by a network of empty roads and narrow pathways down to the water's edge.

42-43
Flat Valentia Island has been connected to the mainland since 1971 by a bridge. It is the site of the Skellig Experience, a modern building that documents the monastic and seafaring life of the Skellig Islands that lie before it.

44-45
The 19th-century town in the photograph is Killarney, set in a wide fertile valley. The town has little to boast architecturally except for the lovely Neo-Gothic cathedral of St. Mary's whose bell tower can be seen at the bottom right.

44 bottom
The broad port of Dingle is protected by the slopes of Ballysitteragh. The port was at its busiest during the 16th-century when it had a fruitful trading relationship with Spain. Today, the local economy is based on fishing and tourism.

45 top
Enclosed by lakes and
mountains and blessed with
a mild climate, Killarney is a
small though busy tourist
town which first started
attracting admirers in 1750
after the fourth Lord Kenmare
ordered the construction of the
first carriage road.

45 bottom
The small town of Listowel
was built on the river
Feale and celebrates two
great passions: horse
racing, at its local course,
and culture, at the May
Festival of Writers.

46-47
The largest of the three
Skellig Islands, Skellig
Michael, lies nine miles off
Iveragh peninsula. Remains
of an early Christian
monastic settlement on the
island can be reached via
narrow flights of steps cut in
the rock.

47
Uninhabited for a long time,
the Skelligs are a marvelous
natural reserve thanks to
their favorable climate. Tens
of thousands of gannets
come here each year to lay
their eggs.

48-49
Off Lamb's Head halfway
between Iveragh and Beara
peninsulas, Scariff Island lies
at the entrance of the
Kenmare river, a deep inlet
that offers safe harbor to
sailors.

50
Farms and pastures stretch as far as the edge of Rough Point, the offshoot on Dingle peninsula that extends into Tralee Bay. Rough Point is protected by the Seven Hogs, a handful of small islands just off the coast.

51 top
The sandy beach in front of the village of Kilshannig faces the Atlantic Ocean in a semicircle from Rough Point to the sea town of Fahamore.

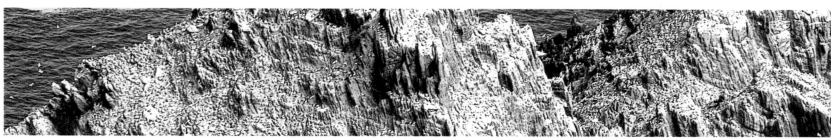

51 bottom
The neat order of shapes and colors along the coast of County Kerry reflects the age-old combination of land and sea, stockbreeding and fishing, that has always been the basis of the life and economy of the island.

52-53
The inaccessible spires of Skellig Rocks form a fragile but protected natural habitat for the many colonies of sea birds that nest in its cracks. The thousands of gulls that live there are particularly visible from June to August.

54-55
The flat countryside of County Clare unexpectedly gives way to a stretch of sandy beaches and rocks scalloped by the wind.

CLARE

A NATURAL SPECTACLE

54 bottom
An enormous promontory slowly advances against the waves. This is one of the marvels of County Clare, where caves and grottoes on the desolate promontories offer safe hiding places for migrating wildlife.

55
On its slow advance towards its estuary, the river Shannon widens and breaks up into hundreds of "callows," meadowland that is difficult to cultivate but suitable for drying out hay.

56
Iridescent streaking and sandbars line the wooded banks of Ireland's largest river until it joins the waters of the Atlantic.

57 top
Moss, lichen and the occasional tuft of grass are the undisputed masters of the slender sea stack that stands in front of one of Ireland's most famous natural landmarks, the Cliffs of Moher.

57 bottom
As sharp as blades, the rugged promontories that shape the shoreline near Kilkee emphasize the uncontested superiority of natural forces along the west coast of the island.

58-59
The spectacular and simple Cliffs of Moher form a lookout station five miles long. These cliffs of schist and sandstone are some of western Ireland's most popular tourist destinations and offer wonderful points for observing guillemots, puffins and herons.

60-61
The modern road that winds past Bunratty Castle does not affect the mystery of this square fortress built by the MacNamara family. It is surrounded by fine grounds in which typical historical dwellings of farmers and fishermen have been reconstructed with original furnishings.

61 top
This ancient stone lookout tower monitors the coast of County Clare where it meets the plateau of the Burren. The tower offered a reassuring presence on this stretch of coast that in war and peace was always a favorite landing place for vessels from all countries.

61 bottom
O'Brien's Tower is the
name of the round building
that overlooks the Cliffs of
Moher and from which, on
a clear day, it is possible to
see the Aran islands and
the hills of Kerry and
Connemara.

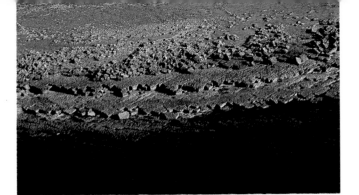

62 top
Similar to the more northern
Connemara, the coast on the
boundary between County Clare
and County Galway is a sequence
of huge boulders and enormous
expanses of stratified rock.

62-63
This bare landscape carved by concentric terraces is typical of the corrugated plateau of the Burren, a limestone platform that lies between Ennistymon and Ballyvaughan.

63 top
There are few roads across the rocky desolate Burren. A few routes follow the coast from Doolin to Bally-vaughan before turning in-land towards Lisdoonvarna.

63 bottom
In contrast to its apparent aridity, the bare expanse of the Burren conceals various types of flora in its nooks and crannies. Here you will find examples of Arctic, alpine and Mediterranean species able to survive thanks to underground waterways.

64-65
The peaceful flow of the main course of the river Shannon mingles with tributaries from between cultivated and marshy areas. In the past, the river was an important trading route and the scene of many religious settlements.

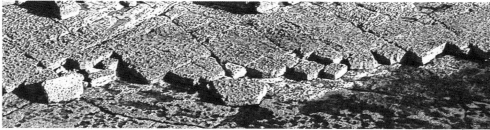

GALWAY
GENTLE WILDERNESS

66
This is a view of Clifden, the largest town in Connemara. Each year in the middle of August, horse dealers from all over Ireland congregate at the horse fair here to celebrate the qualities of the sturdy Connemara pony; evening entertainment of jigs, ballads and beer is provided in the local pubs.

66-67
19th-century Kylemore Abbey was a wedding gift from an English magnate to his bride but looks older than its Victorian origins. The abbey faces a small lake and is now a convent for the Sisters of Ypres who transferred to this remote corner of the west of Ireland from Belgium after World War I.

67 bottom
The private church of
Kylemore Abbey is hidden
among trees and bushes of
rhododendron and fuchsia
close to the lake and the
main body of the convent.
The church is a miniature
Neo-Gothic reconstruction of
York cathedral.

68-69
The 16th- and 17th- century
architecture of multi-story
Dungaire Castle and its

encircling stone wall was
restored in 1954. Today the
castle is the setting for
medieval banquets.

69 top
This is the wreck of a merchant ship battered by the waves on the rocky shoreline of Inisheer. It is not an unusual sight on the rocky islands that form the Aran archipelago off the coast of Galway.

69 bottom
At first gentle and home to thick vegetation, the coastal landscape of Connemara soon turns wild and bare. The wild beauty of the west of Ireland between Galway Bay and the fjord of Killary Harbour has entered literature.

70
*This view of cliff
stratification on the island
of Inisheer, the smallest
of the Aran islands, reveals
its geological similarity
to the limestone plateau
of the Burren from which
it is separated by just
a short stretch of sea.*

71
*Inishmore is the largest
of the Aran islands. It has
three villages: Kilronan,
the main harbor for the
island; Kilmurvy, which
lies along a lovely beach;
and Killeany, which gives
its name to the island's
largest bay.*

72-73
Dry walls mark the
boundaries of the small
properties on Inisheer.
Each stone commemorates
the effort of the islanders to
make the land arable;
to do so they imported
soil from the coast of
Galway which was strewn
in layers with sand
and seaweed.

73 top
Solitude and a supernatural
quiet make the Aran islands a
land of legends and sea stories.
Life on the archipelago has
inspired writers and directors,
in particular the American
Robert Flaherty who filmed
"Man of Aran" here in 1934
which described
the harsh conditions of
life on Inisheer.

73 bottom
The wharf on Inisheer
extends into Foul Sound,
the stretch of water that
separates the island from
Inishmaan. The ferry is the
only way for the islanders
to reach the closest island
or the small port of Doolin
on the coast of the Burren.

74-75
These are the two faces of
Inishmore: on one side an
inaccessible rocky mass and,
on the other, Killeany Bay
with the village of Kilronan
that is the major tourist
center on the archipelago.

$\mathcal{M}$AYO

THE MAGIC OF THE PAST

76
Fjords and lagoons ring the coasts of Blacksod Bay in the extreme north of County Mayo. Note the peat bogs at the top that show signs of recent extraction.

76-77
A radiant landscape of bright colors signals the jagged headland of The Mullet. In 1588, the largest ship in the Spanish Armada, La Rata Encoronada, sank here off Blacksod Point.

77 bottom
One of the many inlets
of Blacksod Bay. The
view portrays the two
natural elements – land
and sea – that form the
basis of Ireland's raw
beauty.

78-79
The tiny farms that crown The Mullet overlook the scenery of Blacksod Bay, where narrow tongues of sand are sprinkled with shells and molluscs at each retreat of the tide.

79 top
An uninhabited land of supernatural simplicity lies outside of Bangor, the ancient baronetcy of Erris, where important archaeological remains have only recently been discovered below the protective layers of peat.

79 bottom
The dappled marshlands
that stretch from Bangor to
Crossmolina mark the
boundary of the area
known as Erris and named
after the family that once
owned it.

80 bottom left
This is another view of
Blacksod Bay and shows
the irregular and desolate
tracts of land that seem to
want to float away on the
waves with the first breath
of wind.

80-81
Laceworks of earth and still
water form the basis of the
coloring of this almost
unpopulated area of County
Mayo. It is an open-air
quarry for those needing
supplies of peat.

84-85
Elegant Ashford Castle was originally built in the 13th-century but expanded in 1872. Now it is a hotel in a park on the outskirts of Cong. The entire area, castle included, was used as a film set in 1952 for John Ford's "The Quiet Man," starring John Wayne.

82-83
Strong sunshine slightly blurred by haze throws an aura of mystery over this tiny cemetery on the shores of Lough Corrib. The lake is divided between Connemara in County Galway and County Mayo.

83
A round tower tops the remains of the chapel in a graveyard not far from Castlebar, the county capital. The town was founded in 1613 during the British colonization but was later destroyed by Irish rebels.

86-87
The whole of County Mayo
appears to face away from
Ireland toward the ocean
(seen at the top of the
photograph). Its idyllic
countryside summarizes the
magic and Gaelic spirit of
Ireland.

87 top
The tides decide the passing of the boats along the canal that connects Blacksod Bay with the bay of Broad Haven. This waterway was dug at Belmullet, a small town built at the base of The Mullet.

87 bottom
The photograph shows Belmullet's position between the two marine bays. The canal in the foreground allows ships to move the short distance without having to put out to sea and round The Mullet.

88 bottom left
A palette of liquid greens and blues forms the small islands that emerge from the surface of Lough Carra. One of these islands is the last resting place of George Moore, whose ashes were placed in a mound tomb.

88 top right
Pasture lands and lakeside vegetation edge the shores of Lough Corrib where amateur and international fishing competitions are held.

88 bottom right
Lough Carra's shallow waters are ideal for safe anchorage and swimming. The peaceful scenery offers excellent walks along the water's edge.

89
To the north of Lough Mask, another lake, Lough Carra, was the inspiration for George Moore's short story "The Lake." Moore lived for a long time at Moore Hall, the ruins of which can be seen on the west bank of the lake.

90-91
Downpatrick Head sticks out into the waves of the Atlantic like the tip of a spear. A local legend says that the Head was the scene of a challenge between St. Patrick and the Devil.

90 bottom
Sitting atop the cliffs that dominate Blacksod Bay, one of the 80 lighthouses still in operation around the island waits for night to fall. Four lighthouses have been placed under the protection of the Irish Landmark Trust and will shortly be converted into tourist accommodations and information centers.

91 top
The jagged coast of County Mayo between Bunwee and Downpatrick promontories remains an undiscovered area of the island. Covered by a second skin of peat and rock, it still conceals remains of prehistoric sites.

91 bottom
One mile off the Atlantic coast of The Mullet, a stumpy lighthouse protected by wind barriers has dominated the rocky summit of Eagle Island since 1835.

92 top
Gusting clouds that herald possible rain add drama to this view of the mountainous Mullet taken from Blacksod Bay.

92 bottom
Deep silence and empty shores along the County Mayo stretch of Lough Corrib are enjoyed by freshwater fishermen who consider this lake an angler's paradise.

92-93
The view of Salrock is deceiving. From above it seems like a Nordic fjord immersed in an unreal quiet and hardly disturbed by the energy of the sea and wind.

94-95
The snaking line of land and sea traces the promontory of The Mullet at the point in which it begins to open like a fan towards the Atlantic. To the right, we see Belmullet and the canal that connects Blacksod Bay and Broad Haven.

$\mathcal{S}$LIGO AND $\mathcal{L}$EITRIM

WHEN LANDSCAPE BECOMES POETRY

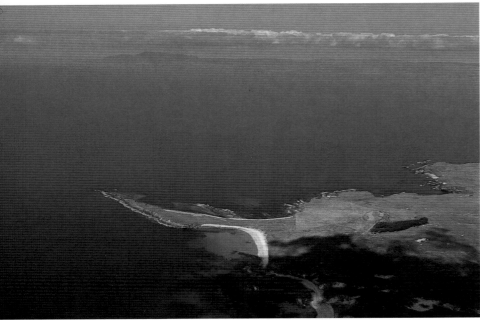

97
The distinct outline of Benbulben is difficult to lose from sight along the bends of the coast. Here it is seen from Rosses Point, the holiday village frequented by William Butler Yeats and his brother Jack.

98-99
Two modes of life are contrasted in this picture that shows one of the most open stretches of the county's shoreline. The boundary is clearly marked between the world of farming and a relatively dangerous life at sea.

96 top
More than a bay, Sligo Bay is a vast gulf with irregular features divided into three separate basins by fingers of land and lined with fine sandy beaches.

96 bottom
The broken coastline of Sligo Bay sometimes falls sheer into the waves and sometimes descends in a natural stairway. Its geological formation is of layers of rocks shaped by the wind.

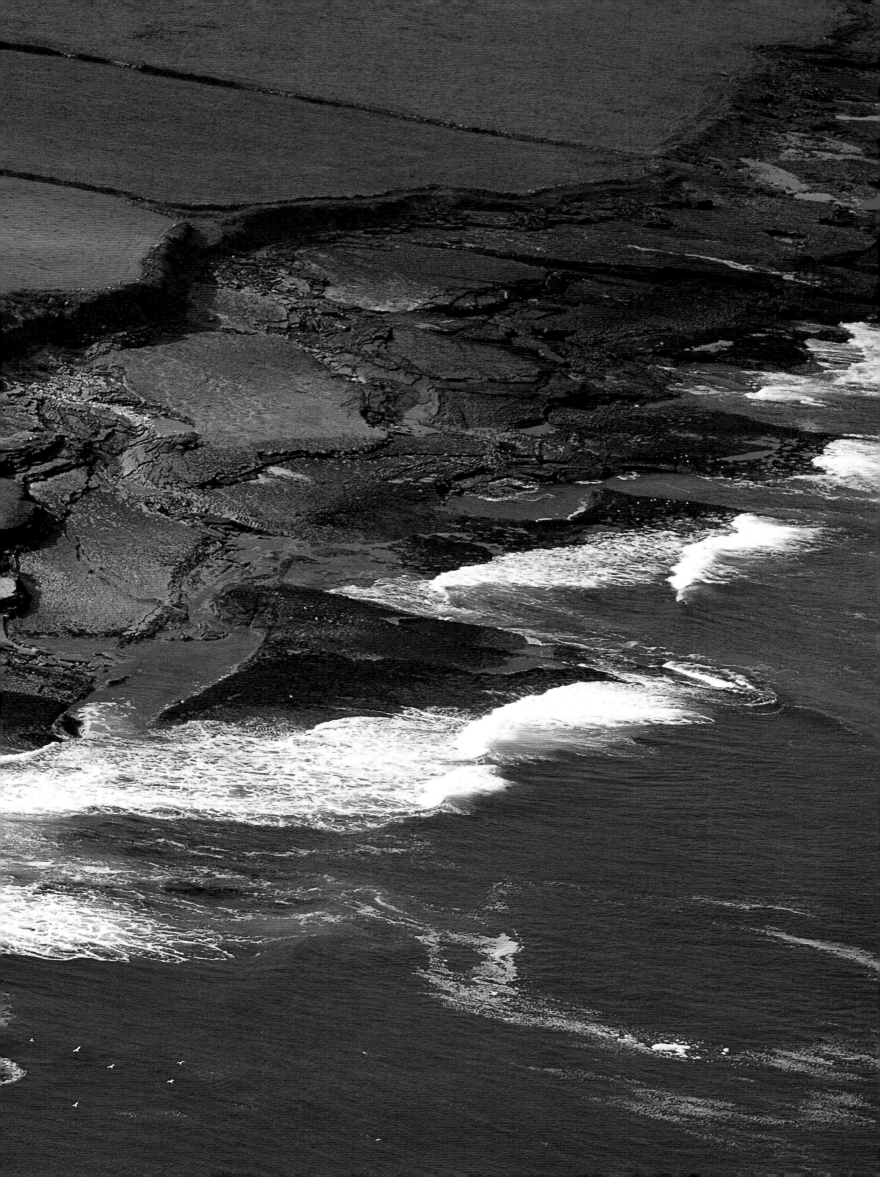

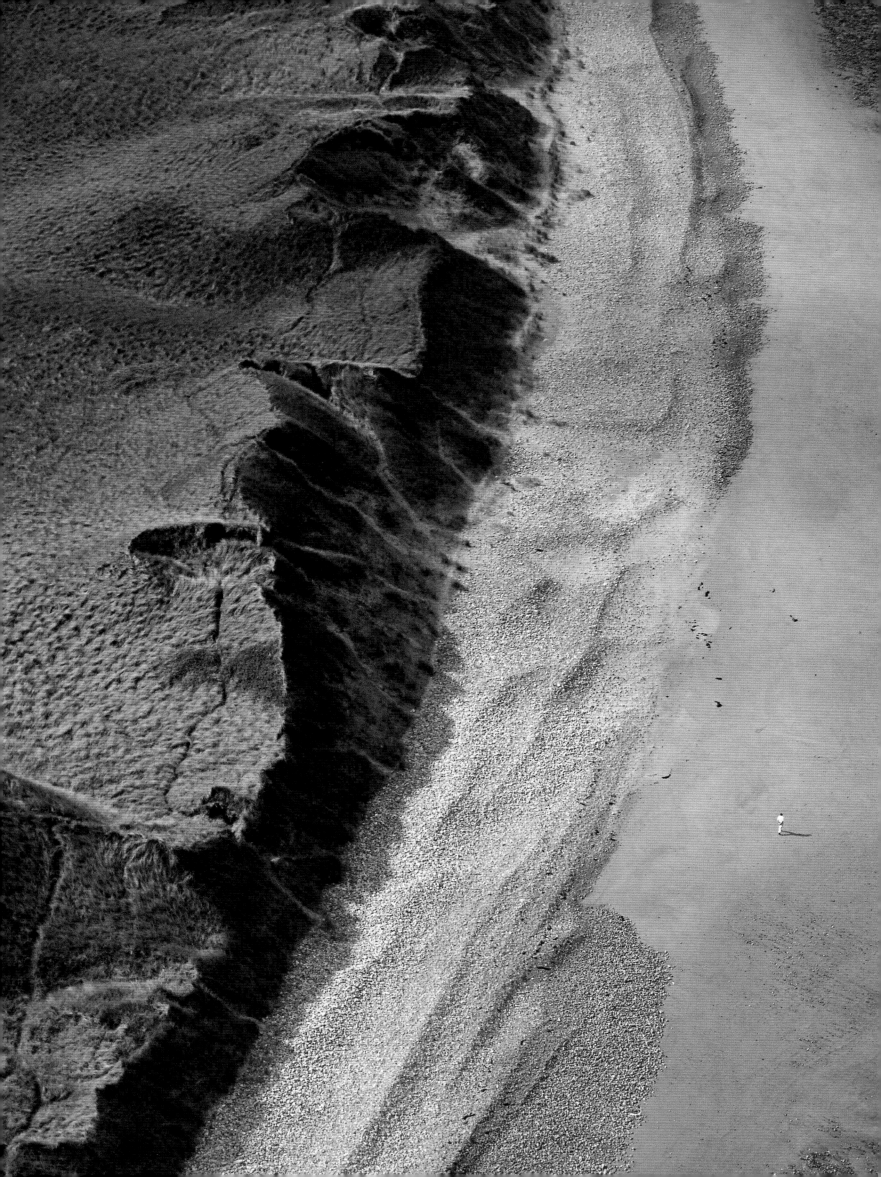

101 top left
Brushstrokes of harmonious colors depict another seascape of Sligo Bay, where man plays only a supporting role.

101 bottom left
Long, ceaseless waves flow over the deserted coastline of Sligo in one of the wildest and most rugged areas of northwest Ireland.

101 bottom right
The mainland seems to float on the blue expanse of Sligo Bay. This is a perfect place to let time slip past, marked only by the movement of the tides.

100
Wave-smoothed pebbles and shells crunch under the feet of those who take an invigorating walk along this beach protected by a line of dunes in this hidden part of the bay.

102-103
The rainbow over Benbulben indicates the possible presence of a leprechaun who is said to hide a pot of gold at the foot of the arc.

103 top
Sandbars in Drumcliff Bay, one of the inlets in Sligo Bay, underline the mass of Benbulben plateau. The ashes of W.B. Yeats were buried in the Protestant graveyard in the village of Drumcliff seen on the shore.

103 bottom
Dunes and sandbars provide an improvised golf course on the shores of Sligo Bay. Golf is a highly popular sport and Ireland has over 400 courses.

104 bottom right
As though it were a mirage created by the sea breeze, the tides and the sun that reflects on the trembling surface of the ocean, Sligo Bay shows the changing nature of its beaches.

105
A light breath of wind helps the tired waves to their destination on the unending beach of Sligo Bay.

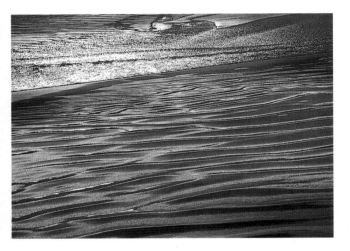

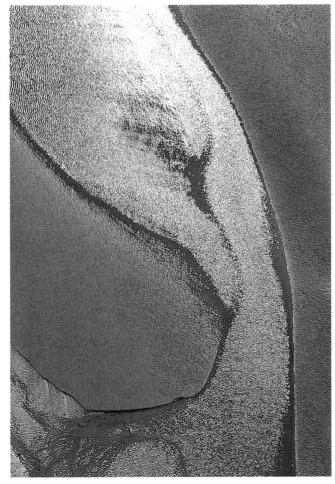

104 left
The waters off the coastline of County Sligo are treacherous; sandbars and shoals revealed by low tides are indicated by lighthouses close to the most dangerous spots.

104 top right
The silky backdrop of waves lulls the mind in Sligo which, more than any other region, arouses deep, soothing emotions with its magic and beauty.

106-107
Galloping horses on the
beach of Sligo Bay: this is a
common image in northwest
Ireland, where pony rides
and walking excursions
offer direct contact with
nature.

106 bottom
A sailing boat heads away from the Sligo coast towards the ocean. Despite the island's long coastline and the richness of its waters, the Irish fishing industry is still young with much room for growth.

107
A sailboat plies the waters of Sligo Bay. Sailing is a popular sport throughout the land and it was in Cork where the world's first sailing club was founded in 1720.

108
Tunnels and underground caves are to be found throughout the crumbling limestone of the Sligo coastline. This has led to the creation of a bird reserve at Lissadell House where several varieties of geese and rare wild birds now live.

109
The vivid green of the fields contrasts with the flat limestone plateau inland from Sligo Bay, the area with the highest concentration of megalithic structures in all of Europe.

110 bottom
Once, the land behind Sligo Bay was covered in forests which allowed the nomadic people of the area a comfortable existence as they moved between hunting, fishing and agriculture with the changing seasons.

110 top
Founded in the 9th-century around the fort that monitored movements between Connacht and Ulster, the town of Sligo was developed by the Normans. Its decline began in 1645 when Oliver Cromwell aided in destroying the town's medieval past.

110-111
The town of Sligo is a flourishing commercial port cut in two by the river Garavogue. The town is strongly linked to the memory of W.B. Yeats, the poet to whom a study center is dedicated.

112
*Encircled by gentle hills,
the perimeter of Lough Gill
is lined by thick woods
and equipped with picnic
areas.*

113
*Tranquil, lying just a few
miles from Sligo, Lough Gill
is the lake that feeds the
river Garavogue, famous for
its trout, pike, and salmon.*

114-115
*In addition to its beauty,
Lough Gill also has cultural
links. It is possible to visit a
lovely restored Georgian
property and the small island
of Innisfree which inspired
W.B. Yeats to write the poem
"The Lake Isle of Innisfree."*

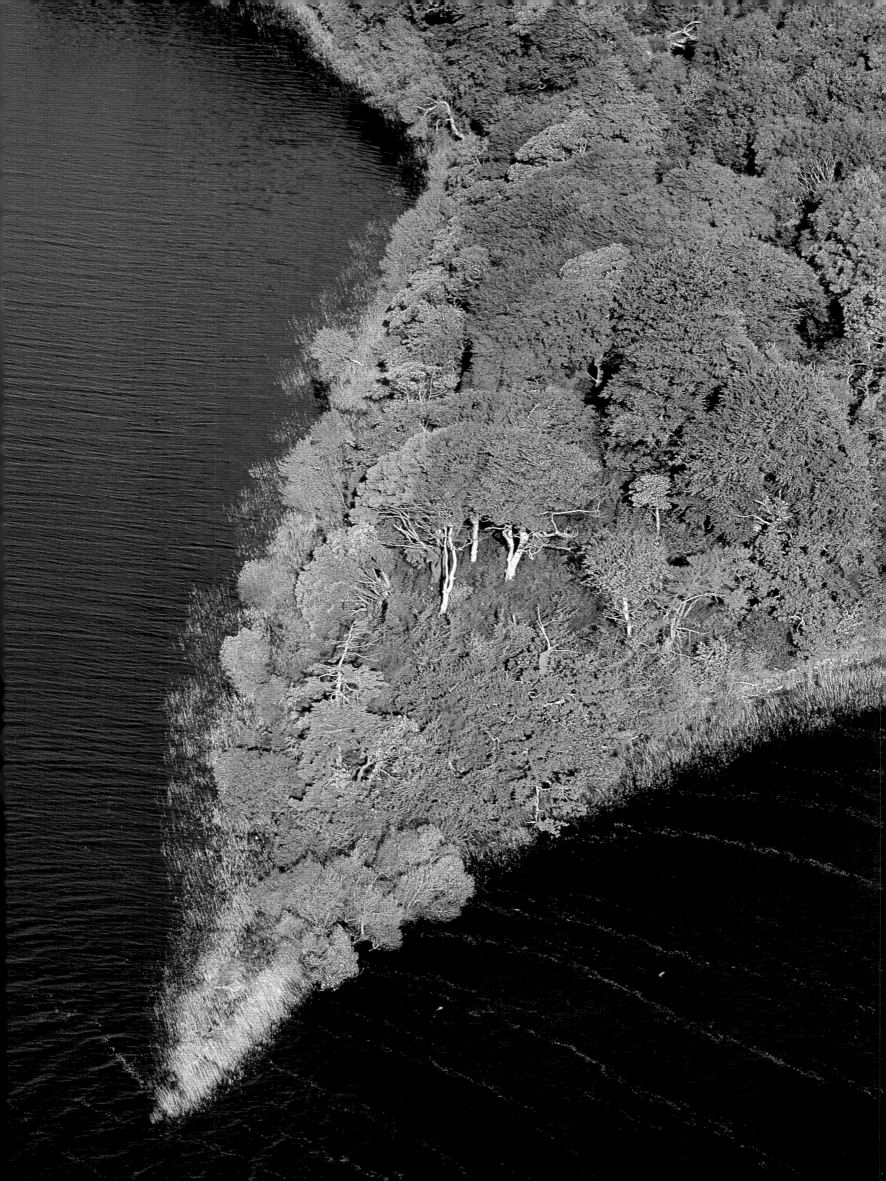

116-117
Varied landscapes, steep hills, ravines and fish-filled lakes are the typical features of this north-eastern county as yet relatively untouched by tourism and ideal for lovers of unspoilt nature.

117 top
A few miles south of Mullaghmore, Classie Bawn Castle is a private property that used to be the residence of Lord Louis Mountbatten, uncle of the Duke of Edinburgh, Queen Elizabeth's husband.

117 bottom
Woods and a grassy mantle cover Lough Key Forest Park on the shores of the lake of the same name. The lough lies in the county of Roscommon which covers some of the ancient estate of Rockingham that until 1957 was the property of the King-Harman family.

118-119
Overlooking a favorite
inspirational spot of W.B.
Yeats, Lough Gill, Parke's
Castle is a 17th-century
square fortress built by
Thomas Parke.

118 bottom
The pleasant port and
fishing town of Carrick-on-
Shannon is enhanced by
unpretentious buildings that
look onto the two main
streets, Bridge Street and
Main Street. One of them,
Costello Chapel, is perhaps
the smallest church in all of
Ireland.

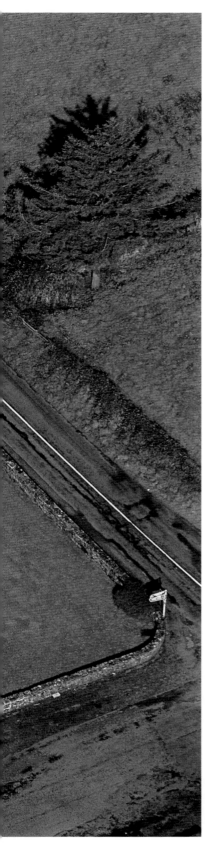

119 top
Facing the sea that has
always provided its
livelihood, Mullaghmore is a
pleasant holiday and fishing
resort that overlooks a
beach more than two miles

long on the south side of
Donegal Bay.

119 bottom
Situated at an important
junction of the country's
river system, Carrick-on-

Shannon is one of Ireland's
largest boating centers. Here
it is possible to hire cabin
cruisers and head off to
explore the 140 navigable
miles of the Shannon's
waterways.

120-121
Narrow sandbanks and
dunes protect the bay of
Mullaghmore from the
capricious Atlantic and offer
protection and shelter to
those who challenge its
currents.

121
The well-defined profile of
Benbulben points the way
for those wishing to reach
the rugged shores between
Sligo and Leitrim and
admire the natural beauty
of the sea and wind.

122

The low coastline with its fine dark sand appears and disappears to the rhythm of the tides. This is the approach to Mullaghmore Head, a lookout point over the whole of Donegal Bay.

123

A strip of land stretches out in the crystal water of Mullghmore Bay, as a challenge to the sea.

124-125

This is a view of Donegal Bay near Mullaghmore. In the background, the plateau of Benbulben is visible many miles away: it is a mystical place linked to myths, legends, saints and hermits.

FERMANAGH

A HISTORY LINKED TO RIVERS AND LAKES

126 top
This is the center of Enniskillen. The winding Main Street is the commercial and economic center of the town. Note the copper dome

of the Victorian Clock Tower in the foreground and the Protestant cathedral of St. Macartin's in the background that was partially rebuilt in 1842.

126 bottom
Standing on the waters of Lough Erne, Castle Coole House belonged to the Maguire family and was a large part of the history of Enniskillen.

126-127
Founded by Captain William Coole, Enniskillen, the capital of the county, stands on an island between the twisting shores of Lower Lough Erne. Its strategic position made it the setting for various power struggles in the past.

127 bottom
Sober Castle Coole stands in the park to the southeast of the city. Designed by James Wyatt, it reflects the essence of Palladian style in that the simplicity of the building's external appearance contrasts with its sumptuous furnishings and decorative interior.

128-129
Green fields and thick woods wrap the islets of Upper Lough Erne in mystery. Many hide the ruins of monasteries and archaeological curiosities.

130 top
Rural, vividly colored landscapes form the northern strip of northwest Ireland, the least-populated region of the country with fewer than 30 inhabitants per square kilometer.

130-131
A sort of five-pointed star rises a few meters from the flat shores of Donegal Bay, offering a safe landing spot.

DONEGAL
A BULWARK OF GAELIC CULTURE

131 top
This is a close up of one of the many remote beaches in Donegal Bay. These tiny corners of paradise are not easily reached.

131 bottom
This sandy shore in Gweebarra Bay is one of the more popular beaches, close to Clooney Wood.

132-133
Donegal Bay reflects a split personality: it is fringed by promontories that stick out towards the restless ocean while, behind, there lies a peaceful expanse of cultivated fields and pretty little beaches.

134 top
The coast of County
Donegal fans out into the
ocean like the claw of an
extraordinary sea creature.

134-135
Slieve League, at 600 meters high, is fronted by the tallest cliffs in Europe. They rise out of the

Atlantic as though they wish to protect the region of the Gaeltacht, the strongest bulwark of Gaelic culture.

135 top
Rocks that slowly disappear into the depths, fields that try to survive the lash of the briny wind, and roads that push their way through the landscape are typical of the headlands of County Donegal.

135 bottom
The contrast of the rugged shore with the soothing grasslands that stretch inland is indicative of the fragile balance of this part of coastal Donegal. The forces of nature produce continual alteration of the environment.

135

136 bottom
An immense lagoon with irregularly shaped tiles in a liquid mosaic interspersed with shreds of land. This is a sketch that cannot, or does not wish to, take shape, molding itself to the more uniform sections of Donegal Bay.

137
Lands sculpted by time and the forces of nature extend placidly to Donegal Bay, an area still searching for a precise identity.

138-139
Narrow passages and sandy banks line the curved shoreline of Loughros More Bay, an offshoot of Gweebarra Bay where Ardara is known for its tweed production.

136 top
Besieged by the sea, a narrow peninsula in Donegal Bay almost seems to want to emerge from the waves. The remains of a few stone buildings lie here as the only indication of previous human presence.

140-141
This is the wrinkled headland that lies just a few miles from the remote village of Malin More at the tip of Rossan Point. It is an area of prehistoric dolmens and Glencolumbkille, the locality linked to the cult of St. Columban.

140 bottom
A rough track along the bay of Malin More leads to the tip of Rossan Point where panoramic views and the lovely Trabane beach can be admired.

141
The forbidding crag of Malin Head forms the tip of Inishowen peninsula to the north of Londonderry and marks the northernmost point on the island.

142-143
A stone fortress protects the cliffs of Malin More from the assaults of the sea. The ruins of a monastery are visible on Rathlin O'Birne Island a short distance from the coast.

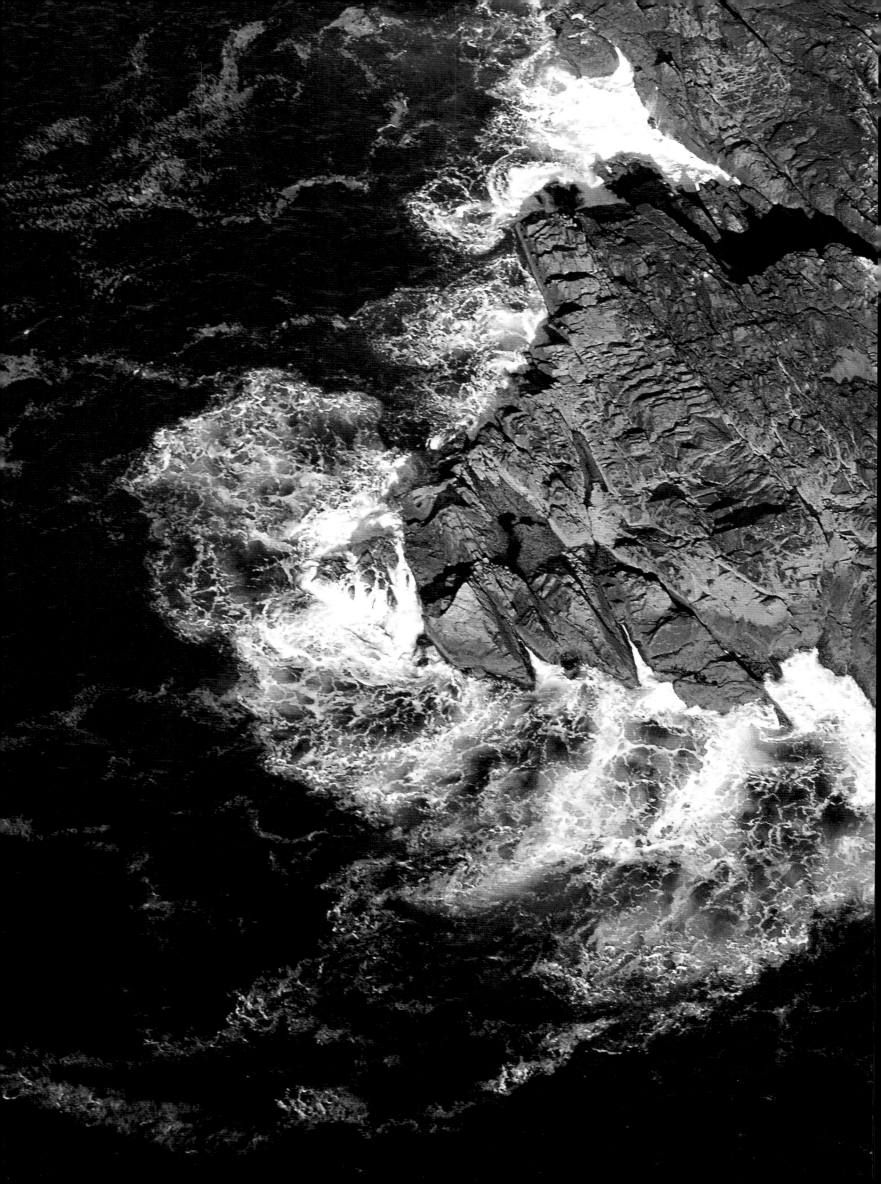

144 top left
The Gweebarra river is a short stretch but of rare beauty. Its turquoise waters run from the slopes of the Derryveagh Mountains in broad curves, leaving sandy bends in their wake.

144 center left
A chaotic mix of colors daubs the final stretch of the Gweebarra estuary in its slow, serpentine advance to the banks of the estuary.

144 right
Lustrous colors of indefinable shades line the last stretch of the Gweebarra river as it prepares to enter the bay that bears its name.

144 bottom left
After a long series of swoops between sandbanks and rocky ridges, the Gweebarra bursts open into one of the loveliest outlets in the Atlantic.

145
The Gweebarra river runs into the sea where it mixes gradually with the saltwater of the long estuary inland from Maas and north of Ardara.

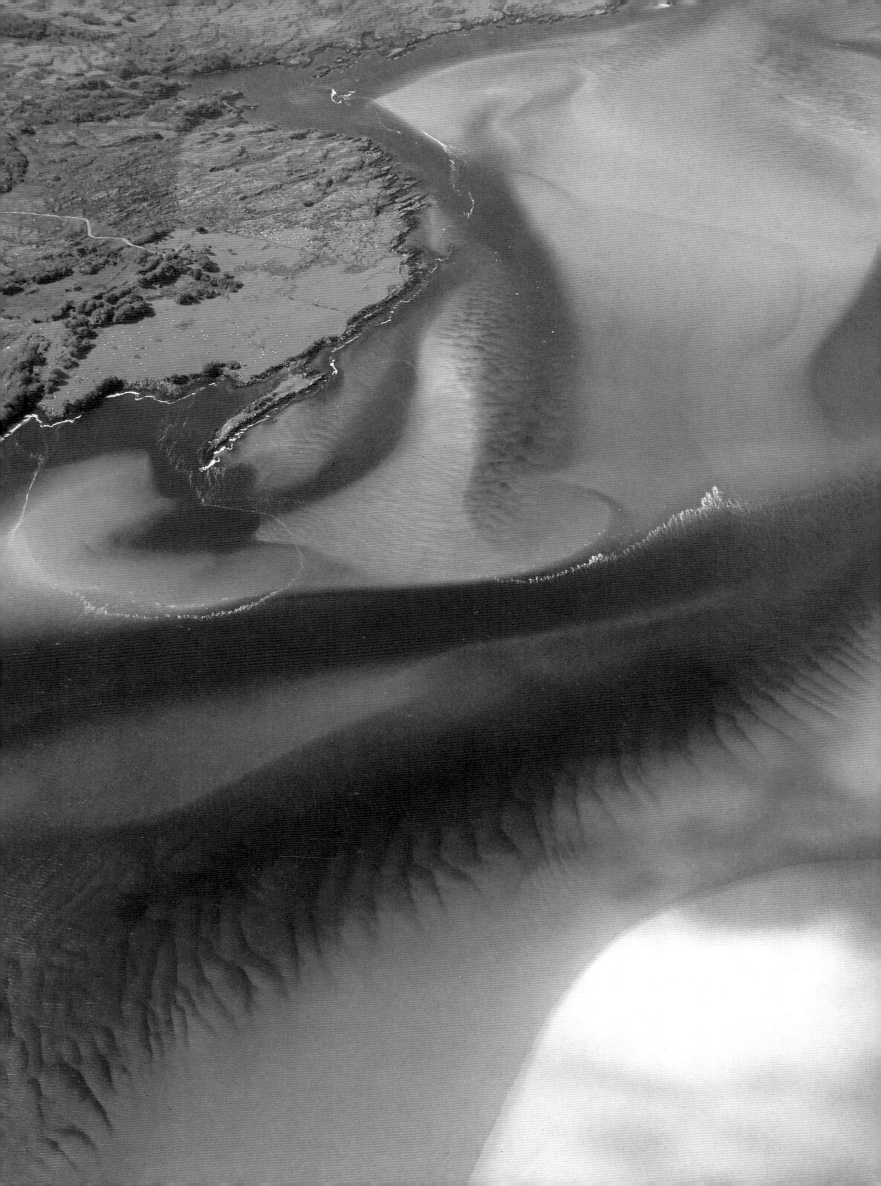

148-149
Hemmed in by the land and the rocks, the upper stretch of the Gweebarra river and its tributaries push their way through the countryside of Donegal, cutting deep and attractive chasms along its banks.

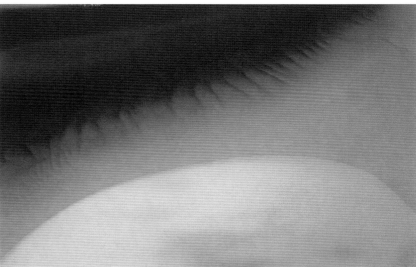

146
Frilly lines of foam trace the water's edge, changing shape with every wave along the undulating shores of the bay and sketching the irregular outlines of a surreal bas-relief.

147 right
The pale colors of the sand change with the movement of the cold Atlantic waves in a sheltered section of Gweebarra Bay.

147 left
Artistic spirals of sand embellish the shores of Gweebarra Bay in a blending of sea and land without equal.

LONDONDERRY
SCULPTED BY NATURE

150 bottom right
The historic residence of
Runkerry House stands on a
hill near Bushmills. It was at
one time a house for the
elderly, then a juvenile reform
school, and has now been
converted into private flats.

151
Standing alone on the edge of
the ridge above Downhill
Strand not far from the
seaside resort of Castlerock,
Mussenden Temple is a small
library that was once part of
a property now in ruins.

150 left
Behind Mussenden Temple,
well-nourished flocks of
sheep graze among the ruins
of Downhill Castle built in
1770 by the fourth Earl of
Bristol, the eccentric bishop
of Derry.

150 top right
The photograph shows the
round Neoclassical
Mussenden Temple and
Downhill Castle standing on
one of the last stretches of
land in Northern Ireland
opposite County Donegal.

152-153
Londonderry stands on the Foyle estuary. Northern Ireland's second largest city, it has a long and controversial history; it still has its 17th-century city center with four main streets and four gates.

153 top
The Georgian town of Limavady lies on the banks of the river Roe. It is the departure point for visits to Roe Valley Country Park, an area to the south of the town where old mills and equipment for bleaching linen are displayed.

153 bottom
The growing industrial
suburbs of Londonderry
have brought much needed
employment to an area of
traditionally high
unemployment.

154-155
*These are the neat, linear
roads of Portrush, one of
Northern Ireland's best-
known seaside resorts,
known for its long sandy
shore and golf course.*

155

*A hem of fine white sand
rings the water's edge of one
of the more remote corners of
the coast of County Derry.
This little paradise has
managed to retain its
original natural habitat.*

156 top
A long strip of asphalt runs without any particular destination through the bogs around Londonderry. Evergreens have recently been planted on either side, in soil impoverished by the progressive extraction of peat.

156 bottom
Summer is the time for harvests and new seeding in County Derry when the land is transformed into a natural patchwork of browns and the greens of the pastures.

156-157
The train runs on the panoramic line between Belfast and Londonderry. It stops at Ballymena and Castlerock before cutting back to follow the coast route.

ARMAGH AND NORTH ANTRIM

LAND OF SAINTS AND GIANTS

158 top
Antrim's pastures offer excellent grazing to the many animals that wander unrestricted even up to the crests of the cliffs. Livestock is one of the island's main resources with 67% of its land used for grazing.

158-159
Profiles of prehistoric animals, spectacular grottoes and arcades worthy of a cathedral are to be seen in the hard chalk and basalt walls along the coast around Portrush at the northern tip of Northern Ireland.

159 top
A country road winds around a simple church and its graveyard. Faith and traditions *are facts of everyday life for many Irish regardless of the progress of society.*

159 bottom
An insignificant fence encloses the coastal pastures of County Antrim. The county is the result of geological upheavals that created attractive bays in the coastline and left extraordinary deposits of lava.

160-161
This high-level view of the countryside around Lough Neagh allows the gaze to wander over an unending expanse of green occasionally marked by darker patches of woods and hedges.

162 top
A stronghold of Christianity, Armagh was the place chosen by St. Patrick when he founded his first church in 447. Since that time, it has been an important center of religious life and fine religious buildings.

162 bottom
This is a close-up of Armagh cathedral, reached by a handsome flight of steps. Inside the visitor can admire stained glass windows by the Dublin school and Italian mosaics and sculptures.

162-163
Curiously, Armagh, capital of County Armagh, is the religious capital of the entire country. In the center of the photograph, the majestic Neo-Gothic Catholic cathedral from the second half of the 19th-century rises above the rest of the town.

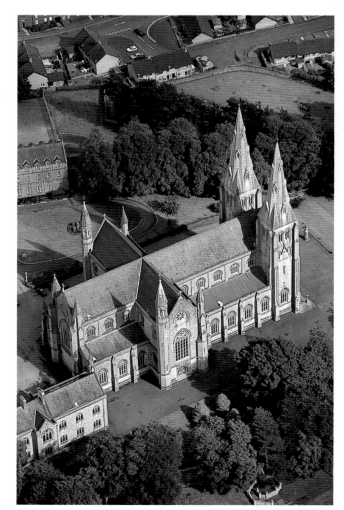

163 bottom
Colonized to a great extent by farmers from Worcestershire, County Armagh is nicknamed the "Orchard of Ireland" and is famous for its Beauty of Bath and Bramley apples.

164 top
The north of Ireland is distinguished by rocky outcrops and narrow clefts. The primordial beauty of the land produces a strong emotional impact.

164 bottom
Moss, brackish water and forms of marine life emphasize the natural beauty of a stretch of Antrim's shoreline. The rocks and small islands were formed by ancient volcanic eruptions.

164-165
A carpet of moss covers the cliffs of Antrim that rose from the water 20,000 years ago at the end of the Ice Age. The British archipelago began to take shape, separated from continental Europe, as the ice retreated.

166-167
Hints of a stormy past and the whispering of the sea breezes through its ruined walls make Dunluce Castle one of Northern Ireland's loveliest attractions. Its secrets and history remain shrouded in mystery.

168 top
The 60 miles of the Antrim coast from Larne to Portrush – at times open, at others jagged – offer a series of wonderful landscapes and reach the height of beauty here at Murlough Bay.

168 bottom
Walkers along the paths of Murlough Bay near Ballycastle are presented with a timeless landscape and a series of tiny beaches to visit.

168-169
Isolated on a crest near the cliff's edge, an old mansion now converted into a hotel offers an invitation to the traveler to relax and enjoy some warm Irish hospitality.

170-171
The first few rays of sunshine break through storm clouds and reflect on the waters of Lough Neagh surrounded by fields sometimes no larger than a domestic garden. The lake has always been of economic and historical importance to the whole of Northern Ireland.

DOWN

IN THE FOOTSTEPS OF ST. PATRICK

172 left
Velvet lawns and quiet ponds surround the clear waters of Strangford Lough. A hundred or so species of fish inhabit it. In summer, seals give birth to their young here.

172 top right
A well-cared-for wood grows in the artificial lake at Hillsborough, a village about eight miles from Belfast that grew around a strategic fort during the second half of the 17th-century.

172 bottom right
One of the solitary beaches in Dundrum Bay almost at the narrow inlet to Dundrum lagoon. This was the first area of Ireland visited by St. Patrick and to have heard his preaching.

173
Long, regular waves break on the sandy shore of Tyrella Beach. Seen against the background of the Mourne Mountains, Dundrum lagoon is known for its strong, cold currents.

174
*The small town of
Hillsborough huddles
around its 17ᵗʰ-century fort*

*and the Governor's Palace,
a Georgian building in a
lovely park of wide avenues
and wrought-iron gates.*

175
*The romantic, turreted castle
of Killyleagh faces
Strangford Lough. The town
was the birthplace of Sir
Hans Sloane, a self-taught
physicist, who was later to
found Kew Gardens and the
British Museum.*

176-177
*The area dotted with lakes
around Strangford Lough is
known as "St. Patrick's
land." This was where the
future patron saint of
Ireland worked as a pigherd
while still a slave.*

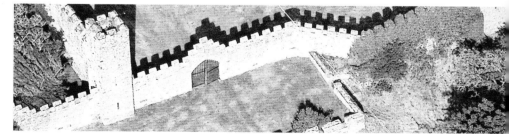

178
Fresh and salt water mix in the rural scenery of Ards Peninsula, a natural barrier between the Irish Sea and Strangford Lough where three Cistercian monasteries stand on the inland shore.

179
Tyrella Beach, awarded the Blue Flag for the cleanliness of its water, is better known for horse riding and walks along its huge sandy beach than for swimming.

180-181
Bordered by dark rocks and the coast road, St. John's Point is a lookout point over Dundrum Bay and lies opposite Newcastle, the village at the southern end of the bay.

182-183
In the hinterland of County Down's flat coastline, a network of walking paths crisscrosses the Mountains of Mourne that rise as high as 852 meters.

184
These are the shallows around St. John's Point, the cape on the headland that was used during the 18th-century for smuggling liquor, silk, soap and tobacco to Ireland from the Isle of Man.

185
Rocks and the shoreline are marked by the tides on a sheltered beach near St. John's Point. This may have been one of the landing places used by the smugglers who then used to disappear into the hills.

186-187
The winding coastline near St. John's Point is another example of the closeness of rural and maritime Ireland, the two fundamental constants in the tormented history of the land and its people.

BELFAST

THE OTHER FACE OF THE ISLAND

188-189
The geographical center of the capital of Northern Ireland is Donegall Square, surrounded by modern buildings, shopping centers, and the Neo-Renaissance City Hall built at the start of last century.

189 top left and right
Once the seat of the Parliament of Northern Ireland, Stormont is now experiencing a new phase as the home of the Northern Irish Assembly, the new governing body that was set up after the peace agreement in 1999.

Stormont Castle was built in severe and uniform style. It stands five miles outside of Belfast in large grounds in the center of a major geometrical road junction.

189 bottom
That Belfast looks to the future can be seen on the banks of the river Lagan, where economic development has been the result of recent years of relative peace. The circular building in the foreground is Waterfront Hall, a theatre and concert hall.

190 left
As one flies over Belfast, the curved Palm House stands out to the south of the university district. The building is a large conservatory in the Botanical Gardens in the Northern Irish capital.

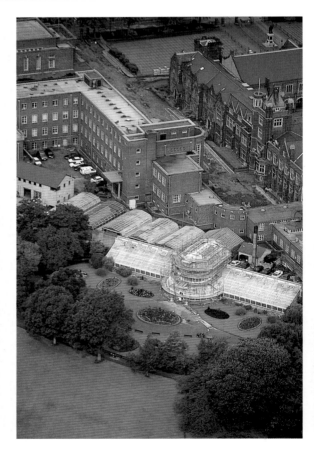

190 top right
Red-brick Queen's University was originally a simple college but was elevated to university status in 1908. Over the past century its educational success has won it international awards.

190 bottom right
Sloping gently down to the banks of the river Lagan, Belfast's Botanical Gardens date from 1827 when the local horticultural and botanical association decided to allocate an area for the cultivation and study of exotic and regional plants.

190-191
This is an overall view of Queen's University, built in 1849 in Tudor style by Charles Canyon. In addition to its educational activities, the university also hosts cultural events.

WESTMEATH
THE CROSSROADS OF THE NATION

192 top
Open countryside, ancient monastic sites and an occasional village are the companions of the Shannon from its source in the Cuilcagh mountains to the estuary.

192 bottom
Christ the King is the name of the Catholic cathedral in Mullingar, the largest town in the county.

192-193
Athlone is a quiet town in the center of the island where the Shannon flows into Lough Ree.

194
Lough Owel lies not far from Mullingar between the Shannon and the Royal Canal. It is a favorite haunt of birdwatchers and is also known for its abundance of trout.

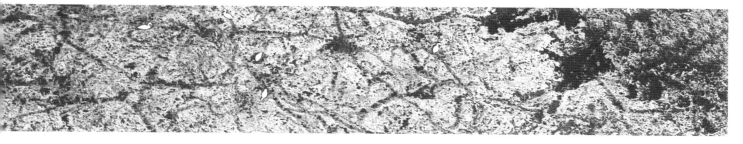

195
Lough Owel is of great ornithological interest. A nature reserve on nearby Lough Iron run by the Wildlife Service is where hundreds of geese from north America spend the winter period from October to April.

196 top
Reeds form a closely-stitched tapestry on the shores of Lough Kinale, a lake near the pretty village of Finnea on the banks of the river Inny.

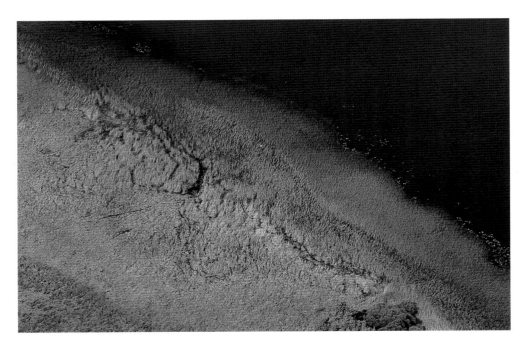

196 bottom and 197
A crown of water vegetation winds around the shores of Lough Owel heightening the aesthetic atmosphere. The same is true of St. Brigid's Well, a spring a short distance from the lake that can be reached by a paved path.

199 top right
To the north of Athlone, Lough Ree is at the dead center of the island, and is known for its trout and many islands, and its 15 miles of waterways.

199 bottom right
The Shannon plays a continuous game of hide and seek with the countryside as it flows in a long series of bends around meadows and fields on its advance through the heart of Ireland.

198
An unpaved road disappears into the waters of Lough Kinale, revealing the signs of recent rain. The lake has a twin, Lough Sheelin, from which it was separated by a famous bridge built in the 17th-century at Finnea.

199 top left
Silence closes over the farmlands of County Westmeath along the banks of the river Shannon. This central area of Ireland is dominated by water, especially after the spring rains.

Agricultural fields, peat bogs, hedges and rows of trees are typical of the flat countryside of Laois, the only county to have retained its Gaelic name and spelling.

OFFALY AND LAOIS

PAST REGALITY AND THE SCENT OF PEAT

200-201
The forested Slieve Bloom chain of mountains is over 500 meters high and marks the boundary between the counties of Laois and Offaly.

201 top
Halfway between Portlaoise and Roscrea, Mountrath is an obligatory stop for those wishing to explore the Slieve Bloom mountains.

201 bottom
45 miles of unpaved roads and mountain paths cross the Slieve Bloom mountains through valleys, woods, glades and waterfalls far from the usual tourist routes.

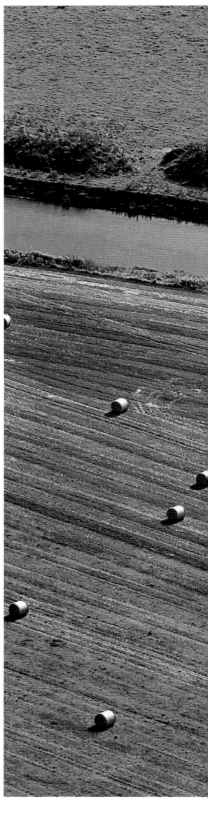

202 top
Streams and canals crisscross the country in a system fundamental to the collection and supply of rainwater. They are especially important to the inland counties, which have always been linked to agriculture.

202 bottom
Peat covers most of the county like a second skin and is a valuable source of energy. It was once used purely for domestic purposes but is now used in industry and collected by Bord Na Mona, the government body that supplies the electric power stations.

202-203
Harvest time in Offaly, the region known since ancient times as "Umbilicus Hiberniae" (the center of Hibernia) as it marks the geographical center of the country.

204-205
The orange Irish Rail train seems never to want to stop as it crosses from Dublin to Galway, bisecting the country and passing from the agricultural east to the magnificent vistas of the west.

DUBLIN

AN ANCIENT BUT YOUTHFUL CAPITAL

206 top left
The seaside resort of Sandymount is one of the quiet suburbs that line the coast south of the capital.

206 bottom left
The slender stem of an obelisk pokes out of the trees in Phoenix Park, created on lands that originally belonged to the priorate of Kilmainham.

206 top right
The district north of the Liffey used to be an industrial and residential area for workers. Today there are plans for the transformation of disused factories and warehouses into shopping centers and modern living quarters.

206 bottom right
This is busy O'Connell Street, the most important in Dublin, where it meets O'Connell Bridge, which is said to be as wide as it is long.

207
Past and present meet face to face in the center of the ancient capital in the shadow of the City Hall. In the foreground we see Christ Church, the cathedral founded in 1038 by the Vikings.

208 top
The centers of learning and finance face one another on the corner of Dame Street and Grafton Street. The square perimeter of Trinity College at the bottom of the picture stands opposite the curved facade of the old English Parliament, now the Bank of Ireland.

208 bottom
A view of Trinity College and the buildings that house the dormitories, libraries and clubs of the students. This is a city within a city, where roughly 10,000 students are taught each year by a highly qualified staff in a relaxed atmosphere.

208-209
This is an overall view of Trinity College in Dublin, the oldest and most prestigious university in Ireland and one of the most highly regarded in the world. It was founded by Queen Elizabeth I of England in 1592.

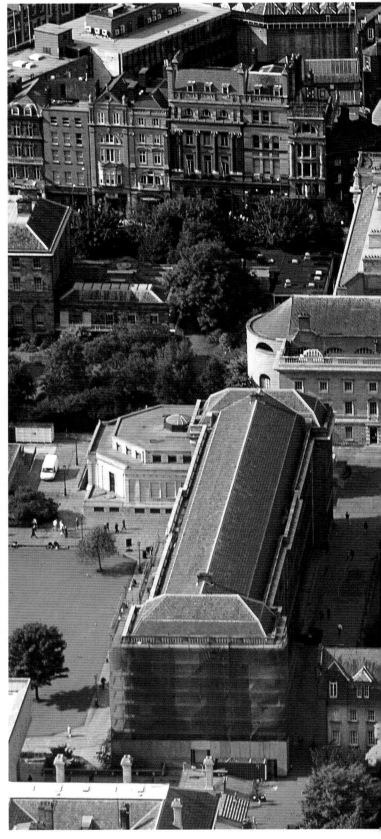

209 top
The strict and imposing buildings of Trinity College have produced dozens of philosophers and men of letters over the university's 400 years of existence. One of the college's greatest treasures is the Book of Kells in the Old Library. The Book of Kells is the gospel thought to have been illuminated at either Iona or Kells by monks that followed the teachings of St. Columban.

210-211
Built on the estuary of the Liffey, Dublin is the size of a provincial city. Despite its rapid growth over the last decades, the city still has large parks, and the houses seldom exceed five stories.

213 center
The small port of Malahide
seems a typical holiday
destination. White terraced
houses with pointed roofs
and seaside promenades line
the seafront.

212
Wrecks of merchant ships
and fishing boats break the
surface of the water off
Malahide, a small town
north of Dublin known for its
stone castle, now a museum,
that was long the residence
of the Talbot family.

213 top
Standing on the point of a
promontory, Howth is a
renowned seaside resort with
a crowded port. The photo
above shows the ruins of
Abbey Church, a small
abbey that was founded
by the Vikings.

213 bottom
The broad panorama of
residential Malahide well
represents the relaxing
atmosphere of the seaside
suburbs north of Dublin.
They are popular on
weekends with city residents,
and are slowly attracting
tourists from abroad.

214 top
Almost halfway between Dublin and Drogheda, Skerries is a busy fishing village with a mild climate. From here it is possible to reach Red Island, St. Patrick's Island and other small islands along the coast that contain archaeological remains.

214 bottom
Its lovely position on the coast and the stretch of land towards the open sea make Portmarnock one of the loveliest golf courses in the country. With over 400 to choose from, the competition is tough.

214-215
Not far from the airport between Malahide and Howth, Portmarnock is one of the most popular golf courses for Dubliners. Besides the course, the private estate also offers a hotel and a conference center.

216-217
Open stretches along the coast to the north of Dublin where quiet villages of cottages are strung together. Lively pubs and excellent restaurants offer Dublin Bay shellfish that is famous the world over.

WATERFORD

ECHOES OF A DISTANT PAST

218 top
This is a view of the south coast of Ireland near Dunmore East. It is characterized by wide green plateaus that suddenly drop into the sea as a result of erosion of the land by the tides.

218 bottom
The handful of houses in Dunmore East are scattered along the waterfront at the entrance to the fjord of Waterford Harbor. Many still have traditional Irish thatched roofs.

218-219
The attractive village of Lismore lies among the woods in the Blackwater valley. At the centre of the photograph you can see the castle at the entrance to the village; originally built in the 12th-century, it is now a private residence.

220-221
The towered medieval castle of Lismore, elegantly rebuilt in the mid-1800s, is open to the public. The avenue to its beautiful gardens is lined with centuries-old yews.

221 top
Lismore's Protestant cathedral stands near the castle. The compact design of the 1633 building is lightened by the slender bell tower. The graveyard still contains 17th-century graves and gravestones.

221 bottom
Puffs of cloud sail over the river Blackwater, one of the most popular stretches of water for trout and salmon anglers.

CORK

THE GASTRONOMIC HEART OF IRELAND

223 right
Recognizable for its tower,
the Anglican church of St.
Ann's in north Cork is
known most of all for its
eight bells, which inspired
the famous tune "The bells of
Shandon" in 1836.

222-223
This is Mizen Head, the
headland at the southwest tip
of Ireland. Right on the tip you
can make out a white
building; this is a coast guard
station and is reached via a
suspension bridge.

223 top left
Financed by the Protestant
families of Cork, the Anglican
cathedral of St. Finbarr's is a
Neo-Gothic building. It was
erected between 1862 and

1876 and marked the split
between the Church of Rome
and the Church of Ireland.

223 bottom left
Don't let the apparent peace
of Youghal, the small town
on the Atlantic at the eastern
boundary of County Cork,
deceive you. Youghal was
occupied by Norman pirates
and later passed to the Anglo-
Normans before being
transformed into a fortified
port by Edward I in 1275.

224 top
Seen from a low angle, the
golf courses near Cobh
resemble sections of
prehistoric settlements.
Throughout the whole of the
country, there are plenty of
opportunities to practice your
swing, and Cork alone has
five courses.

224-225
Youghal was a famous seaside resort in the 1800's and can boast fine and important buildings, but a curiosity is that it is linked to Sir Walter Raleigh who, some believe, introduced the potato to Europe here at the end of the 16th-century.

225 top
Enjoying the last rays of the sun, houses on the edge of Cobh, the city of Cork's naval base since the 18th-century, preside over the ruins of a stone fort surrounded by trees.

225 bottom
Cobh's gray cathedral stands out against the pastel facades of the houses along the seafront. Cobh was the last contact with their native land for many Irish emigrants who departed from the port to the four corners of the world. It is the first contact with Ireland today for tourists who arrive by boat from French ports.

226-227
At one time the port of Cork, Cobh only readopted its original Gaelic name in 1920. Originally it was known as Cove, but after a visit by Queen Victoria it was renamed Queenstown in her honor.

228-229
The river Lee is divided in two by the island that forms the center of the city of Cork. In the 18th-century, the island was split by dozens of canals that gave the city the nickname, the "Venice of Ireland."

230 top
This is a detail of the lighthouse on Galley Head surrounded by its white wall. It can be reached on foot along one of the many coastal paths that follow the jagged shore between Kinsale and Baltimore.

230 bottom
The unceasing waves of the Atlantic assault the slender profile of Fastnet Rock that lies off Clear Island. Every two years since 1925, it has been the turning point in the international Fastnet sailing race.

230-231
The promontory of Galley Head to the southwest of Clonakilty is dominated by this lighthouse. This is the starting point for a tour of the headland, accompanied only by the sound of the breaking waves.

233 bottom
Between Galley Head and Seven Heads, the uniform coastal plateau of Clonakilty Bay is split by deep fissures. The nature of the land and the dearth of traffic make it a natural sanctuary for rare migrating birds.

232
This view is of Mizen Head, that dominates the ocean from a height of over 200 meters. The magnificent headland has no paved roads and is a popular walking area.

233 top
Another dramatic picture of Mizen Head and the rocks at the base of the promontory. It stands at the confluence of the waters of the Atlantic and the Celtic Sea and for centuries was the scene of numerous shipwrecks. Even today it is not an easy passage for expert sailors.

234 top
*High over the inlet of
Dunmanus Bay, a small
farm surrounded by
cultivated fields and country
roads gives a rural air to the
southwest coast.*

234 bottom
*The gentle grasslands of the
region of Cork, known as the
"vegetable garden of
Ireland," give way to rock
until they are lost among the
thousands of splinters of
Dunmanus Bay. Considered
one of the most scenic inlets
in the southwest, it is not far
from the "Ring of Kerry,"
one of the most popular
tourist trips in the country.*

234-235
*A tiny patch of grass on the
last rocks at Mizen Head is a
sign of the vitality of the
land despite the constant
attack of the sea.*

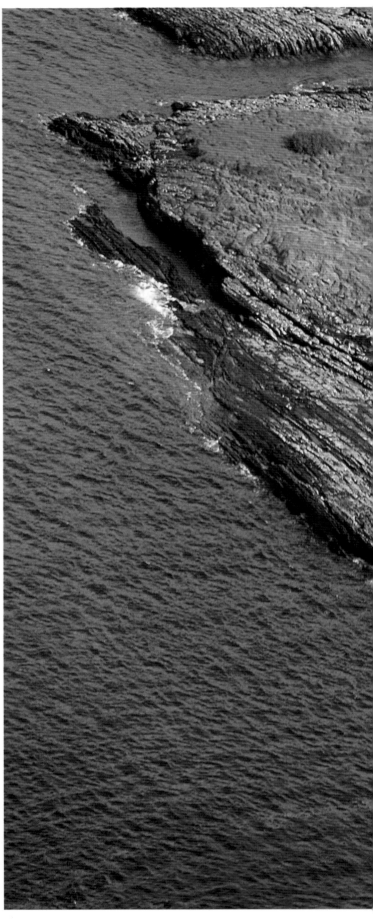

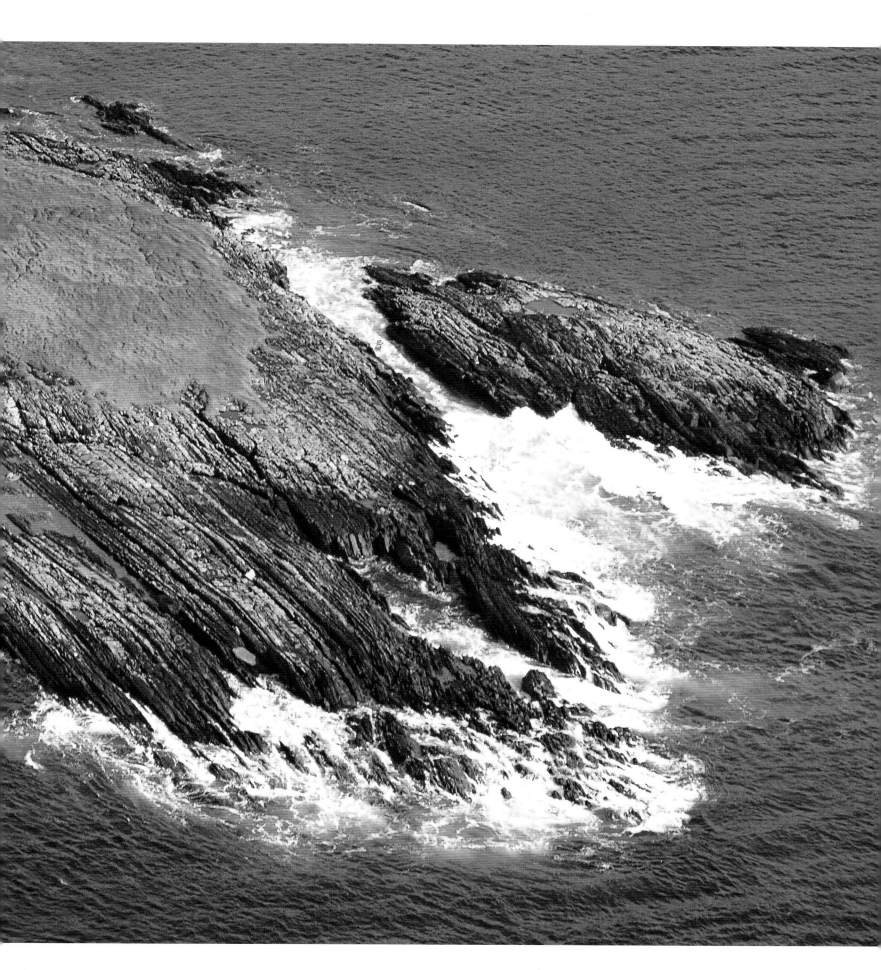

*236-237 Sunny and blessed
by the warm currents of the
Gulf Stream, Bantry is a
seaside town set against a
backdrop of gentle hills that
lies beside a deep bay dotted
with tiny islands.*

INDEX